BRITAIN'S MOST NOTORIOUS HANGMEN

TRUE CRIME FROM WHARNCLIFFE

Foul Deeds and Suspicious Deaths Series

Barking, Dagenham & Chadwell Heath
Barnsley
Bath
Bedford
Birmingham
More Foul Deeds Birmingham
Black Country
Blackburn and Hyndburn
Bolton
Bradford
Brighton
Bristol
Cambridge
Carlisle
Chesterfield
Cumbria
More Foul Deeds Chesterfield
Colchester
Coventry
Croydon
Derby
Durham
Ealing
Fens
Folkstone and Dover
Grimsby
Guernsey
Guildford
Halifax
Hampstead, Holborn and St Pancras
Huddersfield

Hull
Jersey
Leeds
Leicester
Lewisham and Deptford
Liverpool
London's East End
London's West End
Manchester
Mansfield
More Foul Deeds Wakefield
Newcastle
Newport
Norfolk
Northampton
Nottingham
Oxfordshire
Pontefract and Castleford
Portsmouth
Rotherham
Scunthorpe
Shrewsbury
Southend-on-Sea
Southport
Staffordshire and the Potteries
Stratford and South Warwickshire
Tees
Warwickshire
Wigan
York

OTHER TRUE CRIME BOOKS FROM WHARNCLIFFE

A-Z of London Murders
A-Z of Yorkshire Murders
Black Barnsley
Brighton Crime and Vice 1800-2000
Durham Executions
Essex Murders
Executions & Hangings in Newcastle
  and Morpeth
Norfolk Mayhem and Murder

Norwich Murders
Strangeways Hanged
Unsolved Murders in Victorian &
  Edwardian London
Unsolved Norfolk Murders
Unsolved Yorkshire Murders
Warwickshire's Murderous Women
Yorkshire Hangmen
Yorkshire's Murderous Women

Please contact us via any of the methods below for more information
or a catalogue
WHARNCLIFFE BOOKS
47 Church Street, Barnsley, South Yorkshire, S70 2AS
Tel: 01226 734555 • 734222 • Fax: 01226 734438
email: enquiries@pen-and-sword.co.uk
website: www.wharncliffebooks.co.uk

Britain's Most Notorious Hangmen

*The lives and executions of the
'turn-off men'
from Jack Ketch to Albert Pierrepoint*

Stephen Wade

First published in Great Britain in 2009 by
Wharncliffe Local History
an imprint of
Pen & Sword Books Ltd
47 Church Street
Barnsley
South Yorkshire
S70 2AS

ISBN 978 1 84563 082 9

Typeset in Plantin and Benguiat by
Phoenix Typesetting, Auldgirth, Dumfriesshire

Printed and bound in England by
CPI UK

Pen & Sword Books Ltd incorporates the Imprints of
Pen & Sword Aviation, Pen & Sword Maritime,
Pen & Sword Military, Wharncliffe Local History,
Pen and Sword Select, Pen and Sword Military Classics and Leo
Cooper.

For a complete list of Pen & Sword titles please contact
PEN & SWORD BOOKS LIMITED
47 Church Street
Barnsley
South Yorkshire
S70 2AS, England
E-mail: enquiries@pen-and-sword.co.uk
Website: www.pen-and-sword.co.uk

Contents

sir h. d. ingilby bart
  i sherif of york
    the castle
     york
      yorkshire

Sept. 12th 1883

to be forarded
    to the most grave and revent senior i sherif of york George
Watson apply for the ofis of publick exectutner in the place of
the most revered and late lamented mr marwood if your iness
appoints me i will give satisfactshun to all parties conserned
speshally the unappy criminels which will now nowt if your
iness appoint me promp tenshon like shall be my moto and a
post mortal after as will show the unappy criminels insensitif.
if your iness wish i will com and visit yu for a few days like and
explain my principl. as the guverment will have somat to sa wich
is libral in this matter yu will elp me if you tel em i is a libral
twas awful last electshun fittin agen downses all by myself like
samy rowlanson will tell you ow he was were he was thro me and
gladston likes a man like me kindred sperit like hoopin yu will
give me a erly hanging for which yu will be responsible and your
petitioneer will evur pray hoopin we may both life long and hang
together

      i am
        yours affectionately
          George Watson age 27
          labrer
          Castleton
          Grosmont
          York.

Copy of George Watson's application to assist the famous hangman William Marwood.
Lincolnshire Life

Introduction

Sir Thomas Browne, in his book, *Lydford Journey* (1644) wrote:

Oft have I heard of Lydford law,
How in the morn they hang and draw
And sit in judgement after.

Browne was writing because he had heard of a judge of the Stannery at Lydford in Devon: a man who it was said hanged a fellow at midday and then conducted the trial. British history teaches us many things about the moral and legal codes which have created the spirit of the nation, and many of these formative habits and attitudes are anything but pleasant. We have always been a nation fond of exercising judicial killings. In February 2008, the *Sun* would have us believe that little has changed in this respect; the newspaper reported that 99% of its readers wanted the return of the hanging judge and the scaffold.

The feature reported that several famous people wanted the return of hanging, including Anne Widdecombe and David Davis. But interestingly, Sara Payne 'mum of murdered schoolgirl Sarah, nine, is against the death penalty..' the paper stated. The tone of the entire feature was one that has been repeated thousands of times in the media, summed up by the words: 'Almost 100,000 *Sun* readers unite today to call for the return of the death penalty.'

What is not so often discussed is the notion of exactly who would supervise and carry out the hanging. The public hangman was the target of hatred, derision and violence through the centuries in which Britain hanged its felons; he was also often made into a celebrity and was of course the subject of morbid fascination. Hangmen feature just as prominently in the exhibits at Madame Tussaud's *Chamber of Horrors* as villains. Even as long ago as 1601, they have been vilified, even by the men they hanged (in spite of being given money to beg that the death be quick). The Earl of Essex, executed in that year by the London hangman, Derrick, penned a ballad upon his life, and he wrote:

Derrick! Thou knowest, at stately Calais I saved
Thy life, lost for a rape there done,
Which thou thyself can testify –
Thine own hand three and twenty hung . . .

The first hangmen were, on the manors and in the towns, paid by both the civil and the religious power-bases, because courts proliferated and several categories of people in high society had the prerogative of hanging culprits in their domain. They were usually rogues themselves, as was the case with a London hangman observed by a diarist called Machyn in 1556, who noted that 'The 2nd day of July was rode into a cart five unto Tyburn [the hanging site near today's Marble Arch]. One was the hangman with the stump-leg – for theft. The which he had hanged many a man and quartered many, and had many a noble man and other . . .'

Of course, since capital punishment was abolished in Britain in 1964, we have become acutely aware of the sick and revolting adverse views of the act of hanging: notably the death of a person later proved innocent of the capital offence. Such was the recent case of Alfred Moore, a Huddersfield man who was hanged in 1951 for the murder of two police officers. The *Yorkshire Post* for 1 January 2008 announced:

A former detective has uncovered evidence that casts doubts on a man's conviction for murdering two police officers more than fifty years ago . . . At his trial Moore, a poultry farmer with a lifestyle beyond his legal income, admitted carrying out burglaries but said he was in bed at the time of the shootings. The murder weapon was never found.

Detective Steven Lawson had investigated the case and found strong evidence that the real killer was a local man who died in 1998.

In 1961 Leslie Hale wrote a book called *Hanged in Error* in which he looked again at eleven cases of executions for murder and argued that they were almost certainly executions of innocent people. Hale wrote:

Official complacency was given another jolt in 1953. In October, a young police officer on duty in Marlow, Buckinghamshire, was savagely attacked by three men, and left gravely, and it seemed, mortally injured. The officer recovered. In January 1954, three men were brought to trial, found guilty, and sentenced to ten, seven and four years' imprisonment respectively. Had the officer succumbed to the injuries, one or more of them would certainly have hanged. Doubts crept in. The prison grapevine whispered the names of the real culprits, one of whom confessed. The Home Secretary entrusted the enquiry to distinguished officers of Scotland Yard who, pursuing it with commendable determination, established the innocence of the convicted men.

Of course, whether innocent or guilty, the fact is that large numbers of people have been hanged, either at the London Tyburn or in the provinces, over the centuries, and their stories provide high drama, sensation and often darkly humorous entertainment. But the hangman in those dramas of the scaffold is often a shadowy figure, simply mentioned in passing. The name Dick Turpin is very well known in popular culture and history, but how many people know his executioner – Thomas Hadfield? He is prominent only if something goes badly wrong. Many of the hangmen of England have had a drink problem or been severely depressed or even had notably unstable personalities; some took their own lives. On the other hand, some hangmen enjoyed their notoriety and took to the media or to travelling shows when their official careers were over.

The question of why felons were hanged is another that needs to be answered. Albert Pierrepoint, who had hanged hundreds of people in his long career, famously said: 'I do not now believe that any one of the hundreds of executions I carried out has in any way acted as a deterrent against future murder.' Statistics indicate that hanging is not a deterrent, in the sense that the instances of murder do not decline in states in which there is capital punishment. Historically in England, the period with the most hangings, when the hangmen made good money from the deceased clothes and payments for swift business at the block or gibbet, was the Tudor era. Between 1536 and 1553, approximately 560 people were put to death at Tyburn.

There is also the odd fascination with the witnessing of hanging. George Orwell, in his essay *A Hanging*, written from his experience in the police in Burma, made a point of writing about the strange black humour of officials when a hanging is part of their professional experience. After the man has been hanged, Orwell writes, 'Several people laughed – at what nobody seemed certain . . . I found that I was laughing quite loudly. Everyone was laughing. Even the superintendent grinned in a tolerant way. 'You'd better all come and have a drink,' he said quite genially, 'I've got a bottle of whisky in the car. We could do with it.'

In many cases, the hangman was a criminal who had received a reprieve for taking up the unpleasant duty of 'turning off' a fellow criminal. His duties involved far more than simply taking care of the scaffold, ropes and drop; he was the man who administered the whip, cleared the streets of swine and generally acted as dogsbody when it came to manorial or town business with regard to punishment. In

Newcastle in the eighteenth century, he was known as the 'whipper and hougher' – he whipped wrong-doers and cut the sinews (houghs) of the swine. He also had to be either tolerant or well paid when it came to indulging superstition and folklore around the corpse of the hanged man. In the *Daily Gazetteer* for 1748, we have this instance:

> *Last Wednesday Richard Biggs, for the murder of his wife, was executed . . . petitions were made to the sheriff to receive the stroking or the laying on of the dead man's hands, with the agonizing sweats appearing thereon, in order to reduce the swelling; and after bearing his hands on their necks whilst he hung, they seemed so well satisfied with the apprehension of a cure . . .*

The great children's author, Hans Andersen, was taken by his parents to see an executioner, and made to drink the warm blood of the dead killer, such was the belief in the efficacy of such things.

The question arises: how did the hangman learn his craft? Until the mid-Victorian period, there was certainly no apprenticeship or training given. Hanging a condemned felon was the responsibility of the county sheriff and if he could not find a hangman, then he would have to do the job himself. Not until the 1880s was there any proper proposal made for the training of the public executioner. Yet in the early days, the men who did this dirty work managed most of the time, though they often had to pull the legs of the victims, or strangle him or her as quickly as possible if the rope failed or slipped.

Clearly, trades involving butchering would provide some of the essential skills of the craft. The first known hangman in London was a man called Cratwell, active in the years from 1534 to 1538; he was said to be 'a cunning butcher in the quartering of men'. To make the task more of a challenge, the Tyburn gallows (copied at York on the Knavesmire) was known as the three-legged mare, and was a triangular affair made to make the hanging of several victims possible at the same time. On one occasion, twenty-four felons were hanged on this, eight on each spar; none of the bodies touched any other.

Hangings were a massively popular public event through the centuries, until 1868 when public executions were abolished. Thousands usually lined the route to Tyburn, and the swelling crowd at the death scene was often raucous, unruly and callous. In the famous case of Courvoisier, who had murdered Lord William Russell in 1840, there was a crowd of 40,000 people waiting to see the villainous butler die. One of these was Charles Dickens, who described the scene and he reflected on the nature of the hangman: 'I came away that morning with a disgust for murder, but it was for the murder I saw done . . . I can see Mr Ketch at this moment, with an easy air, taking the rope from his pocket; that I feel myself shamed and degraded at the brutal curiosity which took me to that spot . . .' Dickens used 'Mr Ketch' as that had become the generic name for the hangman by that time.

The public hangman's role and duties were eventually taken seriously by William Marwood, the Lincolnshire man who introduced the practice of the 'long drop'. Marwood practised with sacks in order to ascertain the right drop for a specific weight, such that a felon would die by asphyxia rather than strangulation. In many cases, in the earlier centuries of hanging, the knot was made arbitrarily, not by the requisite bone and artery for a quicker death. Though Marwood did have some memorable bunglings, these were not so common as errors made by his antecedents and indeed by some of his contemporaries.

Today, from a viewpoint over forty years after the end of hanging in Britain, it is easy to find accounts of the business of hanging: the procedure and the ritual, yet there is very little on the nature of the business on the staff involved. But in the official reports and enquiries it is possible to find sensitive and thoughtful writing on the topic. For instance, in the report of the committee looking into execution in 1953, we have these words on the hangman:

> *At present, any person may apply to the Prison Commissioners to become an executioner . . . But we recommend that sheriffs should vary their selection of executioner so as to ensure that there are always two experienced executioners on the list . . .*

This was important. In Ireland, for instance, the prison authorities had been unable to find a hangman for most of the penal history of the main prisons. In England, there had been plenty of instances throughout the 1920s and 1930s when the assistant only had officiated. In fact, in the last years of Victoria's reign, an inexperienced hangman was allowed to take on an execution at Lincoln prison, simply because he turned up for the job (in place of the expected man) and the work had to be carried out.

The public hangman is firmly entrenched in the popular culture of British history, and he has been the subject of novels, films and poems. His work has entered street ballads, and the entire subject of hanging has been written about by dozens of famous writers, from Oscar Wilde to Alfred Tennyson. But still, there is the man himself, with his ropes and drop calculations, at the end of the newspaper report. He is not centre-stage. This book aims to bring the biographies out of obscurity and tell the tales of the hangmen from the late seventeenth century to the end of capital punishment in 1964, when the whole sorry record of killings ended with a day of two executions, one in Manchester and one in Liverpool.

My thanks go especially to the writers on hangmen who have opened up the best sources to writers such as myself: James Bland, Steve Fielding, David Bentley, Geoffrey Abbot and John Eddleston in particular. Digging for the stories of the hangmen involves spending time looking at obscure memoirs, snippets in old newspapers, and sometimes looking through the ephemera of early true crime. Thanks to the above writers, that task is not quite so daunting as it once was.

CHAPTER 1

The Early History of Hanging

In the medieval period, before the courts and the criminal law were in place with a full national system, and professional officers in the criminal justice system, punishment was manorial or ecclesiastic as well as implemented by the sovereign. Courts administered by the personnel of the lords of manors and by higher churchmen had capital punishment, and of course they had their own places of execution. A few miles from where I sit writing this there is a place called 'gallows hill'. A study of any early ordnance survey map or of previous maps will soon locate several place-names with *gallows* in the wording.

The city of York, for instance, had several gallows, both within the city and in suburbs, with the church controlling most of these. In 1280 a certain John Elenstreng was sentenced to hang on the Ainsty gallows in York; he was a member of the Guild of the Hospital of St John of Jerusalem and, when he had been hanged, his brothers in that organisation took his body for Christian burial. But the story goes that he

A typical hanging cross memorial, at Hindhead. Author's collection

was still alive when taken to the chapel, and his recovery was seen as being brought about by St James. That was a rare case; in most instances, local gallows were busy throughout the centuries, and most of the hangmen are anonymous. The hangman would have been the person who held the whip when one observer in London in 1552 wrote, 'The 13 January was whipped seven women at the cart's arse, four at one and three at another, for vagabonds that would not labour, but play the unthrift.' The hangman was a lowly figure indeed, reviled by most and pitied by few. When he was not hanging he was whipping someone; his only perks were the sale of the ropes and other mementos of the dead, and of course, money given to ensure a swift death.

From the last years of the seventeenth century, after Monmouth's rebellion and defeat at Sedgemoor (1685) and extensive witch trials, the death penalty was extended and what became known as the

St Leonard's, York, close to the main execution site in the eighteenth century. The author

A hanging at Tyburn about 1680. From an old print

Bloody Code was established. By 1688 there was death waiting for perpetrators of fifty crimes; by the end of the eighteenth century the number of capital offences was 220. Obviously, the period of the French Revolutionary Wars and the wars with Napoleon (1790–1815) increased the level of paranoia in the British upper classes and the propertied new middle classes and so new capital crimes appeared on the statute books, such as the 'administering of illegal oaths' which appeared in the Luddite year of 1812.

When a change was considered, opinions such as this expressed by a writer to *The Times* (as recently as 1923) were usual: 'I should like to register a protest against the view that there is a growing feeling in the country against capital punishment . . . Perverted sympathy for murderers and such mawkish journalism as "Move to save the Ilford Lovers" sap the very morals of a nation . . .' Generally in those years of the French wars and after when there was the Chartist movement in England and regular riots, hanging was part of the fabric of life, something similar to a day at the races, and hangmen were popular with the press and the media, as in this rhyme written about William Calcraft in 1850:

My name it is Calcraft by everyone known
And a sad life is mine to you I now own,
For I hang people up and I cut people down,
Before all the rebels of great London town.

For my old friend Cheshire he learned me the trick
And I dine in the clouds tonight with Old Nick,
For the people on earth do use me so bad,
That with tears I could drown them for I feel now so sad . . .

In the period before the Bloody Code and the appearance of men like Calcraft, the hangings would be the responsibility of the County Sheriff, or of the Lord of the Manor, or of course, the abbot for church trials; the actual hanging seems to have been done by anyone who could be persuaded or threatened to do so, but the practice emerged of the hangman for a place being a criminal who took the job to save his skin. The practice was continued on the very simple principle expressed by George Savile, the first Marquis of Halifax, who said, 'Men are not hanged for stealing horses, but that horses may not be stolen.'

The site of the original Tyburn today, near Marble Arch.
The author

In the eighteenth century, the mediation of execution became more streamlined and the publishers took an interest. The ordinary of Newgate (the gaoler who sat with the condemned) became a criminal biographer and 'last dying speeches' became a popular genre. But also, the reporting of hangings steadily became more prominent and detailed. In earlier times, before prisons were equipped with execution facilities, many places would adopt the practice of hanging a felon near to where he committed his crime. A journalist writing in 1850 wrote about some instances of this:

> *It was formerly the usage, when a crime of remarkable atrocity had been committed, to execute the offender near to the scene of his guilt. The minds then exercised on these painful subjects judged that salutary horror would be inspired by the example so afforded . . . Those who were punished capitally for the riots of 1780 [The Gordon Riots] suffered in various parts of the town . . . The last deviation from the regular course was a sailor named Cashman who suffered death about the year 1817, in Skinner Street, opposite the house of a gunsmith whose shop he had been concerned in plundering . . .*

There was always something especially ritualistic in the work of the hangman. At times they were even asked to publicly burn some offensive publication. Such symbolic actions suggest that the hangman was always the embodiment of that curious ambiguity: the Mosaic law of 'an eye for an eye' was at the basis of his work, but at the same time, everyone sensed that he was engaged in judicial murder. But before 1829, in a world in which there were no professional police, but only local constables and inefficient watchmen, there had to be a deterrence. Before the Victorian period, as historian A Roger Ekirch has reminded us in his history of night-time, the dark brought with it horrible fears of violent crime: 'In response to a midnight alarm in a Northamptonshire home, a small mob poured into the streets with forks, sticks and spears demanding the cause of the uproar.' He also notes that in 1684, the whole village of Harleton 'pledged their aid to Henry Preston, a yeoman who feared nocturnal attack by robbers . . .'

In 1701 an anonymous writer published a tract called *Hanging, Not Punishment Enough*. There had to be a horrendous fear extended to those who sought to break the law, and hanging, with the possibility of the body hanging in a gibbet or being sent to surgeons for dissection to follow, should have instilled terror. But the crimes went on, particularly those crimes brought on by sheer necessity, such as theft and poaching as families starved or simply carried on the traditional means of feeding children and surviving.

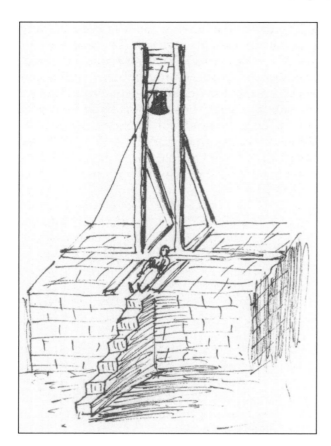

The Halifax gibbet.
Author's collection

Added to the attractions of hanging as a spectator sport, there was the other ritual of the confession. When writer Leman Rede wrote his collection of tales from York Castle in 1869, he ended every chapter with an account of any confession and remorse which took place. A voluntary confession by William Sheward in Norfolk in 1849 gives an example of what these confessions were, and what the interest was in the minds of the public eager for sensation:

On the 14th June, 1851, Mr Christie asked me to go to Yarmouth to pay 1,000 pounds to a captain of a vessel laden with salt.. On Sunday morning I ws going on the above errand when my wife said, "You shall not go. I will go to Mr Christie and get the box of money for myself and bring it home."

With that a slight altercation occurred. Then I ran the razor into her throat. She never spoke after. I then covered an apron over her head and went to Yarmouth . . .

That kind of human drama is at the heart of the history of hanging and of the lives of the notorious hangmen; they were the men who terminated the narratives of the desperate, feckless or sometimes evil individuals who took lives, stole property, set fire to barns or counterfeited the coin of the realm. It was the hangman who closed the last scene, drew the final curtain, as it were, but of course, the players in the tragedy were not actors – they were mostly ordinary people, like the eager crowds at Tyburn, people who made mistakes, took too much drink, or allowed a passion to consume them against all reason. The hangman gave closure to all the issues, moral crises and storms of emotion in the execution tales.

From the earliest phase of history in which the hangman became a professional, there was also the question of the relationship with the accused; the basic requirement was a quick death, and in cases of

*An old illustration to a
very early hanging.*
Laura Carter

treason, when victims were hanged, drawn and quartered, clearly there was little hope of any deal being struck to lessen the agony and terror. But with such deaths as that of women for petty treason (which was the crime of murdering a husband until the 1790s) the normal death would have been burning at the stake, after being dragged on a sledge to the place of execution. It was common practice for the executioner to be given money to strangle the woman before she was anywhere near the pyre.

In some instances, usually with wealthy or notorious felons, there were special requests, as in the case of Captain Montgomery, who took his own life while waiting hanging at Newgate. He had previously requested to meet his hangman. But as the *Spectator* reported: 'By another letter to Mr Wontner, it appears that he was desirous of seeing his executioner on the day before he was to die, a desire, of course, not complied with.' But he avoided the noose. He was found dead in his cell, and the medical men found a quantity of prussic acid in his stomach on dissection.

It says a great deal about the character of the early hangmen when we reflect that, after the Gordon Riots in 1780, one of the condemned was the public hangman, Edward Dennis. After those riots, 135 people were tried; over half of these were transported, and twenty-one were hanged. Dennis achieved immortality because Charles Dickens, in his novel, *Barnaby Rudge,* notably in this passage:

> *"See the hangman when it comes home to him!" jeered one of his Fellow-prisoners.*
>
> *"You don't know what it is, "cried Dennis, actually writhing as he spoke.*
>
> *"I do . . . that I should come to be worked off! I, I, that I should come!"*
>
> *And, uttering another yell, he fell in a fit upon the ground.*

In Scotland, the hangman was called the lockman. In Edinburgh, he was an important civic figure, typified by the life and work of John Ormiston, appointed in 1684. He came from a wealthy family with an estate in Dalkeith, but there had been debt problems, and John was clearly not a man of means, as he started his career in criminal justice as a servant to the master of a house of correction. But he then became hangman, and his executions took place in the Grassmarket. There was a gallows stone there, at the east end of the street. There were also hangings by the Market Cross. We know little about him, as is the case with most hangmen, and detective work needs to be done. Luckily for the historian, there was an account of Ormiston printed in 1834 in

LAST DYING SPEECH

which he is not named but referred to as a gentleman 'of reduced means'.

In keeping with most hangmen figuring in this book, it seems that Ormiston was profoundly affected by his unpleasant work. He almost certainly took his own life; the account of him in *Chamber's Journal* describes this:

> *He would occasionally resume the garb of a gentleman, and mingle in the parties of citizens who played at golf on Bruntsfield Links. Being recognised, he was chased from the ground with shouts of loathing . . he retired to the solitude of the King's park, and was next day found dead at the bottom of a precipice . . .*

Pressing as well as hanging: Margaret Clitherow's house in York. The author

It is obvious that the post of hangman was always a very stressful one. Virtually all hangmen on record developed problems with depression, alcoholism or suicidal tendencies. In 1928, a lawyer called Charles Duff published a little book called *A Handbook on Hanging*, and in it he points out that hangmen were often in danger: 'Towards the end of his career, our own Mr Ellis had personal risk . . . He was often threatened and sometimes had to have police protection, and even to carry a revolver for his own safety.'

In the course of development, there were no real refinements on hanging until William Marwood in the 1870s gave serious thought to making the death less drawn-out and agonising. At the London and York Tyburns it had been a case of using the 'three-legged mare' – a triangular frame made to handle several hangings at once, as happened with the Luddite hangings in 1812–15. The general practice had been to either stand the victim in a cart and then he would hang when the cart shifted, or to have a drop on a scaffold. Hence, with the latter practice, the space beneath the scaffold was available for friends and relatives of the felon to pull on his or her legs and quicken the end. The phrase 'hangers-on' derives from this.

But the noose itself was placed and made with no real thought other than being strong, and of good thickness. The best noose and rope were of silk, and a hangman would sell his silk rope after a hanging, to add to his perks. As to the thought of using a knot to speed the dying process, that was not a main element in matters; after all, a slow death was better entertainment for the crowd. People were in the habit of enjoying the hangings so much that they would book the best seats in nearby alehouses, in advance, to see the hanging. A clear example of this is at Lincoln. In 2007 the massive trees that were growing under the castle walls by Bailgate were cut down, and the visitor today may now clearly see what the view was like from one of the public houses to the hanging tower at Cobb Hall.

In short, the social context to the following biographies of the practitioners of judicial death is one of gut-wrenching terror. The hanging days competed with the racing on the York Knavesmire where Dick Turpin met his end; the crowds lined Oxford Street to shout and jeer

The York prison. The author

A picture of an execution at the York Tyburn c.1799. Author's collection

at condemned people heading from what is now Marble Arch where the Tyburn stood. Today, the historian has to work hard to imagine that terrible location. The gallows stood close to the junction of two roads just a few hundred yards down the road from the Arch itself. Today, tourists sit or stroll around that ground, many having no idea that they are walking on the killing grounds of Georgian England.

To appreciate the reality of what that dreadful and bloody history was, we have to look at the old prints, read the literature, and use the imagination in terms of sheer horrific empathy to even try to understand what it would be like to walk out onto a scaffold and feel the cap drop on the head and the hands tied. But we also have the museums and the heritage industry, from Madame Tussaud's to the prisons. Maybe one of the most powerful statements from that disturbing criminal past is in an inscription written on a cell at Newgate where the infamous child-killer, Elizabeth Brownrigg, was locked up, waiting hanging. It read:

> *For one lone term, or e'er her trial came,*
> *here Brownrigg lingered. Often have these cells*
> *echoed her blasphemies, as with shrill voice*
> *she screamed for fresh Geneva. Not to her*
> *did the blithe fields of Tothill, or thy street*
> *St Giles, its fair varieties expand,*
> *till at the last, in slow-drawn cart she went*
> *to execution . . .*

Her skeleton was on display at the Old Bailey for many years. It is in this kind of gruesome history that the following accounts of the hangmen's lives lie. It is impossible to imagine what it would have been like for a man to perform such killings. Most needed strong drink as well as a firm resolve, and many feared the crowd more than they feared the justice perhaps waiting for them in the life to come.

CHAPTER 2

Jack Ketch

In British history, so strong has been the connection between the name Jack Ketch and the horrors of hanging that the name has become a generic term for the public hangman. He is included in virtually all dictionaries of villains and in fact people with an interest in crime history could be forgiven for thinking that he never existed at all. But we know quite a lot about him, in spite of some confusions in the sources. Jack Ketch in popular culture is so popular that his name even lives on in Punch and Judy shows. His name was used as an instrument of fear for children in the same way that parents would use Napoleon Bonaparte – 'Boney will come and get you!'

The great Victorian historian, Lord Macaulay, said of Ketch that he was, 'a wretch who had butchered many brave and noble victims, and whose name has, during a century and a half, been vulgarly given to all who have succeeded him in his odious office'.

John Ketch lived in Spread Eagle Alley, north of Bow Street, Westminster and was buried at St James's, Clerkenwell. According to a publication of 1679 he was imprisoned for debt at one time, but

The hangman's other skill before the Regency period: using an axe. Popular Educator

A pirate hanged at Execution Dock. Malefactor's Register, 1800

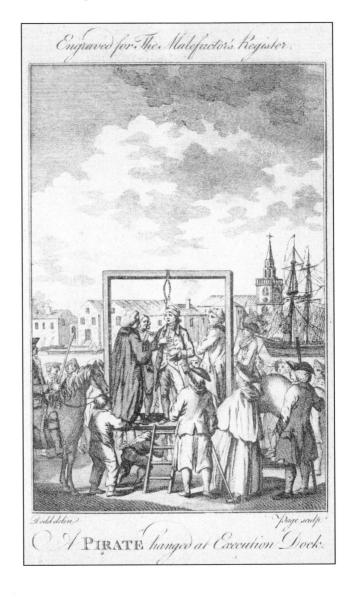

Engraved for The Malefactor's Register.

Dodd delin   *Page sculp.*

A PIRATE *hanged at Execution Dock.*

other statements on his life are questionable, such as the idea that he once went on strike to be given more payment for his essential but unsavoury work. It does appear that he was greedy for money; after a hanging in 1683 Ketch complained at what he thought was a measly fee of three guineas; there was an altercation and he was given more. As was the case with so many hangmen, he certainly knew the inside of a gaol and he was in Bridewell in 1686, sacked and replaced by a man called Pascha Rose. It was once thought that he was reinstated but that is not certain. His life generated many tall tales, including the one that he was really a certain Richard Jaquette, Lord of the Manor of Tyburn – a completely false story probably coming from the world of pantomime rather than social history.

The first references to him are in some publications in print around 1678–9. Whether or not he followed a man called Dunn is not clear, but Ketch was acting as hangman in the years 1678–86, and so he was in office when there was a time of great political upheaval and a number of trials for treason. Unfortunately, Ketch's name is linked forever with the image of the executioner as a drunken, incompetent bungler. But he was definitely involved in hanging the people involved in the Popish Plot of 1678 and the Rye House Plot of 1683; his reputation for barbaric ineptitude comes largely from the mess he made of despatching the Duke of Monmouth to the next life in 1685.

The Popish Plot was hatched by two men, Titus Oates and Israel Tonge, when they came before magistrates in London in 1678 with a massive bundle of lies regarding a supposed Jesuit plot to murder the King, Charles II. The Duke of Monmouth, a Catholic, was therefore allegedly the reason for the plot – that he would restore the Catholic dynasty. Oates was an Anglican priest but he was always in some kind of trouble, and was undoubtedly a petty criminal. He realised that success and status (as well as money and preferment) would come his way if he worked on the plan of inventing a Catholic plot, and in 1677 he became a Catholic, ostensibly to infiltrate the 'enemy'. There was a massive paranoid response to his lies and a genuine plot was feared by many in high office.

Oates pointed the finger at all kinds of men, and this led to thirty-five executions. But if we need to have an illustration of the man at work, we need to look at the case of Lord William Russell, beheaded at Lincoln's Inn Fields in 1683. There were several witnesses there who wrote down their responses, including Sir Charles Lyttelton, who wrote that Ketch tried three times to use the axe, and then still had to saw the remnants of muscle and bone at the neck. Gilbert Burnet was there also, and he wrote that it took two strokes to cut the head.

The most remarkable (and also questionable) source we have about Ketch is from a pamphlet called *The Apology of John Ketch Esq.* Of course, we have no accurate notion of who wrote this; it may well have been what we would now call a 'ghost writer' out to make a few groats by fabricating a biography of a notorious public figure. But it is expressed as a defence: 'Since it is not fit that so public a person as the executioner . . . should lie under the scandal of untrue reports . . .' The work explains the death of Russell and makes every

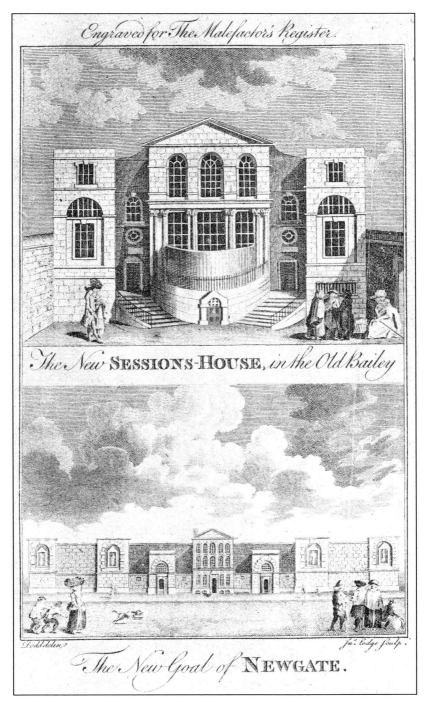

The Old Bailey and the Sessions House. Malefactor's Register, 1800

effort to dismiss the myths and tales, such as the supposed statement by the condemned man:

'You dog! Did I give you ten guineas to use me so inhumanly?' If it is a genuine work, written by the man or at his dictates, then there was a great deal to protest about and to explain. Russell had been involved in the Rye House Plot which had been discovered in 1683: it was a plan to depose and possibly kill Charles and his brother James. They were to be taken at Rye House in Hertfordshire as they returned to London from Newmarket.

We are reminded that the hangman had other duties, when we read that Ketch was the man who whipped Titus Oates all the way to his cell at Newgate, and there is an old print that shows Ketch, well-dressed and smart, using two bundles of rods, like the Roman fascia, with Oates tied to the back of a cart. Oates was whipped further when he was moved again, but he was pardoned in 1689 after serving a few years of what was at first a life sentence for perjury. Ketch clearly felt that he had done well in his career and he had been wrongly maligned.

But it was the occasion of the death of the Duke of Monmouth that really put Jack Ketch into the infamous chronicles of history. After Monmouth's rebellion and defeat at the battle of Sedgemoor in 1685, the trials of the captured rebels were first held at Winchester in August, and the famous 'Bloody Assizes' began. The brutal Judge Jeffreys presided and across the South-West, 300 of Monmouth's supporters were hanged, drawn and quartered. Retribution was extreme and savage; hundreds more were transported to the Caribbean. Jeffreys said openly that any pleas of not guilty would lead to execution; pickled heads and quartered remains of corpses were on show across the land.

Monmouth himself was a client of the horrendous Ketch on Tower Hill on 15 July. It was so widely known that Ketch was incompetent in his bloody trade that the Duke followed the usual practice of giving the hangman money to ensure a quick death. But with Ketch that was not necessarily money well spent. The Duke reportedly said, giving Ketch six guineas, 'Pray do your business well. Don't serve me as you did my Lord Russell. I have heard you struck him three or four times . . .'

Ketch was troubled and nervous. He failed to decapitate Monmouth after three strikes and then said 'God damn me I can do no more . . . my heart fails me!' But he was forced to complete the job, using a knife to sever the last sinews. It comes as no surprise to learn that Ketch was hated. The crowd expected entertainment at the scaffold, and part of that show was to see a clean, swift exit, hopefully after a heartfelt repentance by the felon.

As for the end of the Jack Ketch story, he died at the end of

November 1687, shortly after Rose. If Ketch ever came back to serve again, it was for a very short time. One diarist of the time thought that he had done some work in his last months, writing, 'The 28 May, five men of those lately condemned at the sessions were executed at Tyburn; one of them was poor Pascha Rose, the new hangman, so that now Ketch is restored to his place.' He may well have served for just a few months; it appears that Ketch was buried on 29 November. Little did he know that his record of killings was so horrendous and the fear he instilled so great that his name would live on in British folklore and popular culture for centuries. Arguably he is the most notorious hangman of them all.

CHAPTER 3

John Price

John Price was born in London somewhere around the year 1677, and was at first made an apprentice to a scraps and rags trader. After two years, when his master died, Price did not exactly hang around waiting for developments: he ran away and took up with any trade or general labouring he could. *The Newgate Calendar* author states that 'His mother being left in circumstances of distress, was not able to give him a proper education . . .'

We know that he went to sea as well, putting in service on battleships (men-of-war) and there was plenty of war to be involved in at the time, with the Low Countries mainly. When he came back on land to find a way to start again, it was as the hangman that he found his metier, although the record he left is hardly a proud one.

Price was always in trouble, stepping over the line into lawlessness. But he was also feckless and constantly in debt. This was such a problem that on one occasion, after officiating at an execution of three felons at Tyburn tree in 1715 (the first main Jacobite rising), he was arrested for debt. It is entirely in keeping with the life of the typical Georgian hangman that he just scraped himself out of a long sentence, largely because he had the perquisites of the job: what he earned from sales and tips that day paid his debts. If desperate, a hangman could always sell the clothes of the dead, for example, in addition to selling the rope and having the expected sum to make the 'turning off' swift.

But there were more debts and these dogged him until he was eventually imprisoned in the Marshalsea, in Southwark, described later by Charles Dickens as 'Partitioned into squalid houses standing back to back and hemmed in by high walls duly spiked at the top.' We can have some idea of how grim that place was when we note that one of the warders, a man called Acton, was tried for murder in 1729. But Price had two spells in the limelight of criminal history – first as hangman and then as the hanged man, and his time in the Marshalsea defines the first period. Ketch followed him at that point.

John Price rivals that most infamous of eighteenth century villains in the list of his adventures, Jack Shepherd. This is because he and another rogue escaped from the place; they managed to make a hole in the wall and run for it, after several months inside. But there was a dangerous streak in Price; not long after that he killed a man, in 1718, and then he attacked a woman in Bunhill Fields. This was a very brutal killing. In the *Newgate Calendar*, the account is explicit and savage:

The three-legged mare, York Tyburn. Chris Wade

In the course of the evidence it appeared that Price met the deceased [Elizabeth White] near ten at night in Moorfields, and attempted to ravish her, but the poor woman, who was the wife of a watchman, and sold gingerbread in the streets, doing all in her power to resist his villainous attacks, he beat her so cruelly that streams of blood issued from her eyes and mouth, broke one of her arms, beat out some of her teeth, bruised her head in a most dreadful manner, forced one of her eyes from the socket and so otherwise ill-treated her that the language of decency cannot describe it . . .

Price was tried and sentenced to death. He denied the crime, but there were two eyewitnesses. These people had seen him *in flagrante delicto,* one saying that Price was 'busy about her' and that the poor woman's clothes had been pulled up to expose her flesh. Price had responded to the witnesses' intervention with drunken curses and the words, 'Damn you . . . what do you want?' He had told the people then that the woman was nothing but a drunk. Of course, in court, Price said the usual defensive statement: that he had merely been passing by when he saw Mrs White lying in that awful state. He even claimed that he had helped her to stand and then been found and suspected of the attack. The poor woman suffered a long, painful death, taking four days to die.

John Price was condemned to die. The story circulated in the

Weekly Journal newspaper was that Price was not worried at all by the thought of the noose, and that he went to see the present hangman, took him by the hand and said, 'He had hanged a great many and now he must hang him . . .' The scene took place in Newgate. He was in that gaol for five weeks, in the condemned cell, a place where curious visitors could come, for a small fee, and stare at those awaiting death on the scaffold. The cell would have been dark, extending for around twenty feet by fourteen, and Price would have been constantly shackled in irons.

The *Weekly Journal* reported: 'He hath since sentence . . . been drunk several days excessively and committed horrid outrages.' These appear to have been sexual depravity, and one report states that he raped a little girl who brought him food: '.. the hangman in Newgate

Petty Treason illustrated, a burning of a woman. Malefactor's Register, 1800

has declared that a few days before his execution he had carnal knowledge of her . . .'

He was hanged on 31 May 1718 but at the Newgate gallows: there was no long, ritualistic procession to Tyburn for him. Before the noose was in position, he begged the gathered crowd to pray for him and they hoped that 'they would take warning by his untimely end' and after the hanging he was gibbeted at Holloway. We have an interesting footnote to this, and it tells us a lot about hangmen as a general profession: the hangman who preceded Price was called Marvell, a blacksmith, and he made the iron cover for the corpse on the gibbet. In keeping with the tendency of hangmen to be 'multi-skilled' as we say now, Marvell in retirement still played a part by using another skill.

John Price was just forty-one when he died. Historian James Bland has pointed out a mysterious note on the man's life and story – that a line in the *Weekly Journal* of 28 May, 1720 notes that 'In the same prison died one Price, widow of the late hangman who, had she lived, would have been transported.' That is all that we know of her story. Much of the life of John Price is clouded in legend and half-truth. The facts we know for sure are few. Publications at the time confused his name and story with that of Ketch himself, such was the confusion about the number of executioners working in the last few decades of the seventeenth century.

The *Newgate Calendar* tells his story and ends with a moral assertion: 'The lesson to be learnt from the fate of this man is to moderate our passions of every kind . . .' Price never learned that lesson, and he slid from drunkenness to the lowest depravity, a notorious hangman with a shameful biography, though very much a man of his time in that horrendous criminal underworld of Georgian England.

CHAPTER 4

Richard Arnet

With Richard Arnet, known also as Dick Arnold, we enter the realms of the real survivor in the trade, because he lasted probably a little over ten years in the job. For many years he was one of the most famous, largely because he was the man who hanged two of the most celebrated villains of Georgian England – Jack Sheppard and Jonathan Wild. He supervised a multiple hanging in 1719, something that was always a rare test of a man's nerves of course. He had proved his mettle by the time he executed Wild in 1725.

Arnet's name percolated into the popular literature of the time, but as usual with this profession, the facts of his biography are few. We only really learn any details of the hangmen from this period from their appearances in high-profile events, and Arnet is no exception; in his whipping duties for instance, he was given the task of punishing a man called Moor who had insulted royalty, in 1719. Naturally, such a thing was reported by the press, and it is on record that Arnet had the necessary skill and strength for the job, as his lashes forced the victim to cry out, 'God bless King George!'

But Arnet's name will be forever linked to his despatching of the criminal celebrities of his time. Jonathan Wild was a 'fence' and on a grand scale. He received stolen goods and then sold them, and had a particular skill in selling back goods to the rightful owners. To try to suppress this common practice, the government passed a law to threaten such offenders with the prospect of fourteen years' transportation when convicted, but Wild had a plan of his own. He gathered a large number of known petty thieves, and this is how the *Newgate Calendar* relates it: 'He informed them that he had devised a plan for removing the inconveniences under which they laboured . . . He proposed that when they had gained any booty they should deliver it to him instead of to the pawnbroker, and he would restore things to the owners, thereby greater sums would be raised . . .' Of course, any villain who crossed him would then be 'grassed' to the law, and Wild saw many petty thieves go to the gallows on his information. He even used to advertise his recovery services, as in this announcement from the *Daily Courant* in 1714: 'Lost on 17 March last, out of a compting house in Durham Court, a day book, of no use to anyone except the owner. Whoever will bring them to Mr Jonathan Wild over against Cripplegate Church shall have a guinea reward and no questions asked.'

But eventually the law caught up with him, and he was in fact in Newgate when an indictment against him was opened by the Crown. He had been found out. The theft of a box of lace was his downfall; he was in the process of extorting as much money as he could from the owner (who had come to him for help in retrieving the lace) and she later gave a deposition against Wild. He had maintained a secret correspondence with felons, and he was soon in court, being sentenced to hang on 24 May 1725.

Wild tried to pre-empt the due process of law by trying to take his own life with a quantity of laudanum. But some men worked on him, with exercise and efforts to revive his spirits, and he survived in order to keep the date with Arnet. He 'begged earnestly to be given transportation to the most extreme foot of His Majesty's dominions' but to no avail. When he sat in the cart at Tyburn, Arnet told him that he had a little time to prepare for his fate. But the rowdy, bloodthirsty mob shouted for the hanging to take place. Wild had been stoned on his way to Tyburn. Two robbers were going to die with him and they too were attacked. Arnet had to hang them quickly and curtail the time for the ritualistic speeches and prayers or he, too, would have been attacked.

In 1724 Arnet hanged the notorious Jack Sheppard. This was a man who had escaped from Newgate twice and who had a considerable public following, some of them an adoring group who were to see him to the gallows with some style and noise. Such was Sheppard's popularity that there was almost a very serious riot on his day of death; in the time before his hanging, the ordinary and others had seen the potential in writing about the life of this glamorous character. So we know, for instance, that when the notion of saying prayers was mooted, he said that one file's 'worth all the bibles in the world'.

On 16 November 1724, he was to hang, and he was searched before leaving the Newgate Press Yard, something that did not normally happen. But the officers involved were glad they did so: Sheppard had a knife and he had been planning an escape. Arnet took some time to strangle the life out of the man, and the worst scene in the execution was the trouble over the dead man's corpse. It was the usual habit to give the bodies of felons to the anatomists for dissection. Arnet in fact was paid a retainer by the Company of Barber-Surgeons to supply them with cadavers; he was given a Christmas gift every year, in cash, as a favour for this service as well. But in Sheppard's case, a gang of his friends were at Tyburn to ensure that his body was properly buried. There was a confrontation between the friends and the surgeons, but finally the crowd allowed the body to be taken to Long Acre and, after a wake, it was interred at the St Martin-in-the-Fields' churchyard.

Arnet's tasks in his profession were not limited to the use of the rope. He once had to apply pressing – loading weights on the chest – of a highwayman called Spiggott who would not speak in court. After the torture, he spoke and was duly hanged. But arguably the most horrendous case he had was that of Catherine Hayes. She had murdered her husband, and at the time this was the offence of petty treason, not murder. That meant that she would be burned at the stake. She had bludgeoned her husband to death, with the help of two accomplices, and now she had to die. The usual practice was that a degree of mercy was applied when the woman in question would be strangled before the flames had any effect. The hangman would pull on a rope just as the faggots were lit. When Arnet did this, he was shocked when his hand was burned and he lost the rope. Poor Hayes was indeed burned alive.

But Arnet was generally quite competent. At one time he conducted a multiple hanging at the Execution Dock in Wapping. Offences at sea were usually punished there, hangings being on the off shore at low tide. All these duties Richard Arnet performed capably, unlike so many of his peers. He died in August 1728, and was buried at Deptford Green, at the church of St Nicholas. His obituary reads: 'On Tuesday night the body of Mr Richard Arnold the hangman was conveyed to his house in Deptford . . . The Chief mourners were little Tom, his truly lamenting servant, and his wife . . . and Captain John Hooper is made hangman . . .'

CHAPTER 5

'Mutton' Curry and Askern

I f it came to scouring Britain to find the city that could claim the title, 'City of Scaffolds' then York would be a main contender. Since early medieval times, the place had gallows in all kinds of places, either in the city or in suburbs and neighbouring villages. Not only did the castle and town gaol have gallows, but also the higher clergymen: they organised their own courts and punishments of course. In addition, there were the lords of the manors in the environs of York. Up to the 1890s, even after Armley gaol in Leeds had taken over county responsibilities for hangings, there were still executions at York, in the town gaol, rather than at Knavesmire.

Knavesmire, perhaps more famous for its horse-racing, is the York place-name that always sends a shiver down the spine of crime

Walmgate Bar, York, where felons were brought to hang just a hundred yards beyond.
The author

Where the lucky ones went? Van Dieman's Land (Tasmania). The author

historians. There, not only the likes of Dick Turpin were hanged, but a vast number of other felons, from highwaymen to small-time thieves. Those who did not keep their lives to moulder in the hulks (the prison ships) or to be transported first to America and then to Van Dieman's Land, found themselves in the condemned cell at York Castle prison.

Visitors to York today may still see the prison walls and cells. That dark history has become part of the modern 'heritage' trail and the city has its tourist–centred 'York Dungeons' experience to match that of the London Dungeons. But the hard fact is that, first in the city and then later on the Knavesmire, hundreds of people met their deaths either on a plain scaffold or on the 'three-legged mare' on the Knavesmire. This was a triangular frame, allowing for three villains to be hanged at the same time, and there are old prints in existence that show these hangings. The hangings often took place on race-days, and by the early nineteenth century, when the executions at the Knavesmire began, the good middle class folk of the city and their well-off racing visitors began to complain that the hangings were distracting the crowds from the racing, and also that it was unseemly to have such disgusting deaths going on while others were having fun and quaffing their beer.

Nevertheless, the deaths went on, and the question as to who should oversee the ropes and hoods, the scaffold and noose, was always a tough one. It had never been easy to recruit hangmen. Fortunately, the habit of offering condemned men a commutation of sentence developed, and hangmen were often rogues who did the nasty work to save their necks.

There are two notorious York hangmen in the records: William Curry and Thomas Askern. Curry was also known as William Wilkinson, so matters are somewhat complicated. He was known as 'Mutton Curry' as he had two convictions for sheep-stealing. Fate had been on his side because his death sentences had been commuted twice. He was waiting to be sent to Australia on the second occasion when he turned hangman. In fact he was still a convicted felon, and was a prisoner as well as a hangman until 1814. Curry was to become a true local character – a man with a drink problem, and that comes as no surprise when we reflect on the nature of his work.

There had been no professional training of course. A man who turned executioner had no means of practising his trade other than a knowledge of butchery. If a man had been a farm worker, he would know about tying beasts and he would be skilled with a blade. He might also know a little about weights if he had used a pulley for grain in milling work. But he could only really learn by doing, and that is why, in the twentieth century, after a more rigorous training was in place, dummies were used for drop practice. But in Curry's time it was an occupation with high-level stress and the gin bottle was very useful.

St Margaret's Church, York, where paupers (some of the hanged) were buried. The author

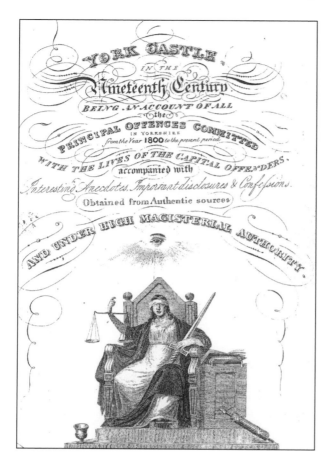

Frontispiece to York Castle *(1829) one of the early true crime books.*

There is some confusion about Curry's real identity. His date of birth was around 1761 but that is not certain. He was from Romanby and his local thefts had led him into deep trouble, first in 1793 when he stole some sheep from an innkeeper at Northallerton, William Smith. Sheep-stealing was a capital offence, and the magistracy took a very serious and often inflexible attitude to that offence. But lady luck smiled on Curry: he was fortunate that his commutation for transportation did not happen; he was sent to the Woolwich hulks. That was obviously far from pleasant, but at least he was not on his way to a penal colony across the other side of the globe. Nevertheless, Curry in his time on the prison ships would have had a very hard time; in the first thirty years in which these hulks were used, one in four convicts died. He would have spent much of his time lifting timber on the Thames shore and when he was not working he may well have suffered the fate of one young prisoner who told an enquiry that he had been in irons while working and sleeping and that he had worn the same clothes for two years. He had also been flogged, and one of the worst cases of abuse there was the case of an old man who had been flogged with a cat'o'nine tails thirty-six times for being five minutes late for a roll call.

But Curry emerged from that, and somehow returned and then at York he took the chance of being the city hangman. What he was called has been a puzzle for historians; one writer gives his name as John; but he was reported as William in 1821 when there was a fairly substantial report on his work. A new drop behind the Castle walls was made in 1802 and it seems that Curry did well, and in 1813 he was the man who hanged the Luddites, so he would come to be recognised. This was a high-profile affair: the machine-wreckers had attacked Rawfolds Mill near Bradford, and it had taken the military and indeed an informer to finally track them down. A new offence of taking at illegal oath was put on the statute book as a capital crime. No less than fourteen felons were hanged at the first session and more were to follow.

Curry has to go down in the records as one of the most capable, because he handled this well and he did the work in two shifts, seven men at a time. The *York Courant* noted that, 'The spectators were not so numerous on the second occasion, owing to the time of the execution being altered from two o'clock to half past one. The entrance to the Castle and the place of execution were guarded by bodies of horse and foot soldiers.' The Luddites had conducted a reign of terror

The death cell at York. The author

across the area spanning Huddersfield and Halifax, and even towards the Lancashire border. They had been fighting the introduction of mechanised shearing, displacing one of the most skilled trades in clothing manufacture.

Unfortunately, whatever his prowess and expertise before 1821, he will be remembered as the hangman who made a terrible hash of executing robber William Brown on that date. Curry had two execution appointments that day, and he had hanged the first victim at the Castle, and Brown was waiting for him at the City Gaol after that. Curry was very tired by the time he reached the second place of execution, and he also 'took a drop' to steady himself. The local *Gazette* has this explanation: ' . . . in proceeding from the County execution . . . to the place of execution for the City, he was recognised by the populace, who were posting with unsatiated appetites from one feast of death to another . . . they hustled and insulted the executioner to such a degree during the whole of his walk that he arrived nearly exhausted . . .'

Curry then had a few drinks to steel himself to the job; he decided to taunt and entertain the crowd by flapping the ropes around and saying, Some of you come up and I'll try it!' After that, he botched the hanging of Brown quite scandalously, as one report said, 'The executioner, in a bungling manner and with great difficulty placed the cap over the culprit's eyes and attempted several times to place the rope around his neck, but was unable . . .' He had prepared the rope too short. It was all becoming more than embarrassing – it was disgusting, though no doubt some of the callous and drunken crowd enjoyed it.

We tend to think of extreme barbarity and extreme sensual pleasure when we consider the media images of the Regency period. But there was plenty of humanitarian concern and conscience as well. In the same year that Curry was bungling at York, *The Manchester Guardian* reported on another hanging with the head, 'Dreadful execution of our fellow creatures':

Before daylight on Tuesday morning a considerable concourse of people were assembled to witness the execution of three of our fellow creatures: Ann Norris, for a robbery at a dwelling house; Samuel Hayward, for a burglary at Somerstown, and Joseph South, a youth apparently about 17. There appeared in him a perfect resignation to his fate, which will be best appreciated by his own words: "I am going to die, but I am not sorry for it – I am going out of a troublesome world." The woman was (as usual) last; she seemed deeply affected. At 14 minutes past eight the drop fell, and they closed their earthly career. When will some mode of punishment be found to save these sacrifices of life?

Mary Bateman, hanged at York. From York Castle (see bibliography).

But the world of 1820 was one sustained by savage repression in all areas. In the Army, in 1822, a private was tried by court martial for stealing a silver spoon from a mess. He was given 300 lashes. Curry was operating in a context of duels, bare-knuckle fist fights, dog-fighting and frequent muggings and robberies on the road and in homes after dark. The mob at York expected something bloodthirsty to treat their vicarious pleasure. With the bungled death of Brown they certainly had that. When at last the felon was dead, people in the crowd shouted, 'Hang him . . . hang Jack Ketch! He's drunk!'

Curry's drinking was clearly an ongoing problem. Later that year, at York Castle, he had the task of hanging five men. But here we have arguably the most farcical event in Curry's career. He did in fact hang the men successfully, but then fell down with them into the drop area. As the local paper reported: 'By an unaccountable neglect of the executioner, in not keeping sufficiently clear of the drop, when the bolt was pulled out, he fell along with the malefactors, and received some severe bruises.' Of course, the crowd were highly amused by that; apparently, 'a shout of joy rose from the crowd' when Curry staggered to his feet and clambered back to the platform. This was all highly embarrassing of course, for the good people of York. But the fact at that time was that hangmen were difficult to find. The authorities persevered with him. The sheriff could easily have dismissed him from the scene then, and of course, he would have been within his rights to sack the man.

Curry retired in 1835 and he was then to be a guest of the Thirsk Parish Workhouse where he died in 1841, aged seventy-six, although there is some doubt about his date of birth. In his career, he had hanged dozens of people, had two convictions for sheep-stealing, and was surely remembered in York history as the drunk who had his tipple of gin to steel himself for his professional duties.

Thomas Askern, another controversial figure, appeared on the scene in 1856, another former prisoner, but in gaol for debt rather than for any violent offence. There must have been the usual deal

Winterbottom (hanged by Curry) depicted in York Castle *(see bibliography)*

done for his release a little time after his appointment, because he was living in Rotherham in 1859. Once again, we have a man whose work was marred by bungling incompetence. He was a man with a varied former career – farmer, butcher, flower-seller, and parish overseer from Maltby. In his time in the debtors' prison he was described as 'a man without money and without friends'.

His first victim was the celebrated William Dove, who had poisoned his wife in Leeds, after a shady involvement with a 'wise man' and quack doctor called Harrison. But, as research by Owen Davies has made clear, there are some doubts about this. Askern denied that he hanged Dove and a minor controversy ensued. Dove was hanged at York on 9 August 1856, after one the most prominent murder cases of the century, and he died in front of a huge crowd of almost 20,000 people. He wrote to Yorkshire newspapers threatening a libel action if they did not withdraw their statements that he had hanged Dove. There was even a letter published in Manchester supposedly from a schoolmaster in York, saying that Askern was not the executioner of Dove. But when traced, the man denied writing it. It seems that Askern's earlier life and hidden debt were indicative of a personality capable of self-deception as well as attempts at deception of others. But some inmates of the debtors' prison wrote to the *Leeds Mercury* to confirm that the man in question was indeed Askern. The hangman had actually attacked one man in the gaol with a stick for saying that he (Askern) had hanged Dove. We have to reflect that perhaps Askern did not want to be linked to a case in which a man died after being the creature of a Svengali-like magician (Harrison) and that there had been posthumous sympathy for Dove, the young farmer and Methodist from a 'good family' in Yorkshire.

In many of his hangings, there were errors and incompetence. It has to be noted that the old habit of giving the hangman cash to arrange a swift death was apparently not still extant at this time, or at least it is not often referred to. There would still be profit from the surgeons of course. But Askern, along with many others at the time, carried on making a mess of things. In a double hanging at Armley a black cloth was put around the victims but still, despite the fact that bodies were out of sight of the crowd, a reporter said that one of the men died quickly but that the other was slowly strangled over several minutes. In 1865, when he was hanging Matthew Atkinson, the rope snapped and the man fell fifteen feet; he was unhurt and stood there for twenty minutes until Askern had a second attempt.

Surely the most shameful bungling of Askern's career was the case of thirty-seven-year-old John Johnson from Bradford. On Boxing Day 1876, fortunately after hangings in public ceased (1868); Johnson was enjoying a drink with Amelia Walker at the *Bedford Arms* in

Wakefield Road; everything was relaxed at first, but Amelia had other men-friends and one of these, Amos White, came into the bar. White made advances to her and she called for Johnson who was at the bar; there was a fight and White was coming off best, but then Johnson ran out, only to return shortly afterwards with a gun. He fired the shotgun at White's chest and then bystanders wrestled Johnston to the ground. Johnson was arrested and charged with murder, and after trial at York Assizes, he was sentenced to die. Waiting for him was Askern. After 1867, legislation was in place concerning capital crimes, and the huge number of such offences before that date was reduced to just murder, treason; the only complications arose when issues of insanity defences arose, or of course, when manslaughter was a possibility. But for Johnson, a crowd of drinkers at the pub had seen him leave and then return with the gun. This was a very clear case of murder and he had to hang for it.

When Johnson was made ready for his last seconds of life, standing on the trap on 3 April 1877, the lever was pulled but the trap broke and Johnson fell through the hole, his feet not kicking air but still firmly on wood. He had to be sat down, groaning on a chair, attended by the gaol warders, who were always ready to help a poor criminal if the death was being handled too slowly and clumsily. Johnson had to be taken to the trapdoor and prepared again. The usual cluster of officials were with him – governor, doctor, priest and sheriff – and the mental preparation for death was experienced a second time, with unbelievably horrific fear running through the man's body. His heart must have been almost bursting through his chest, and whatever resolve he had previously gathered was surely gone as he tried to prepare himself a second time.

It was a total outrage: the drop was only partially successful and his death was slow and horrific to behold. He struggled for several minutes in his death throes. According to one anonymous journalist, writing in the late 1870s, Askern became a man 'shunned and despised and often liable to insults and desperate encounters in public company.' Askern had a final year in office but hanged no one: for the one execution that did take place that year, William Marwood was brought in from Lincolnshire. Askern died in Maltby, at the age of sixty-two, in 1878. After his death, the hangman of England would be national, rather than provincial, with general responsibilities and more media presence. The new hangmen would operate in Ireland as well as in England.

After 1868 executions not being public, the barbaric days at York described by historian G Benson were a thing of the past. Benson wrote: 'York hangings drew crowds from far and near. At such times all the roads to York were thronged. After the railway was opened many came by train and on one occasion in 1856 . . . it was lamented that no cheap excursions were run.' That was Dove's hanging, when thousands from Leeds made the short trip north.

As a coda to the tales of horrendous bunglings on the scaffold, the story of John Thurtell is interesting; Thurtell was due to die in 1824 for the murder of William Weare; he is said to have designed his own gallows, partly through fear of the amateurs in charge. His idea was not adopted but he is on record as having said to the prison governor, ' I understand that when you rounded people here you put them in a tumbrel and sent them out of the world with a *Gee Up* but this is rather an ungentlemanly way of finishing a man . . .'

Thurtell made quite an impact at the time. He was hanged at Hertford on 9 January 1824 and he was written about by Sir Walter Scott; he also has a mention in George Borrow's book *Zincali,* and the artist Sir Thomas Lawrence wanted to make a cast of the villain's head. The novelist Bulwer-Lytton used the Thurtell murder case in his novel *Pelham.* All this shows that by the years of capital punishment reform, in Robert Peel's first ministry, murder survived as the one sensational crime, forever prominent in journalism, literature and poetry. But for Askern, he was doomed to be placed in the annals of hanging as the arch-bungler. No one wanted to include him in their literary works.

CHAPTER 6

Calcraft: Celebrity Executioner

With William Calcraft we begin to encounter the first character who really saw the possibilities of the job with regard to being a public personality. He was born in Essex in 1800, near Chelmsford, and became hangman for London and Middlesex from 1829 to 1874. Although there are some blots on his record, on the whole he was professional. He was the man who hanged some truly notorious criminals in all kinds of major Victorian murder cases, including the Courvoisier murder and the immensely high-profile Norfolk murderer, James Blomfield Rush.

Calcraft was from a poor family with twelve children. William was

William Calcraft.
Laura Carter

Calcraft's trade sign.
Author's collection

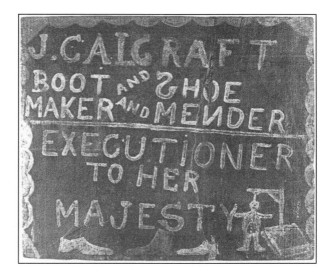

talented and did well at school. When he reached adulthood he was strong and robust, starting out in domestic service, but with an eye for business, he saw that the crowds at hangings would provide a good market for anyone selling food, so he began as a trader in snacks for such occasions. But he obviously saw the executioners at work and eventually realised that he could do the work. An opening came at Lincoln, where he worked as assistant, and then he saw a hangman called Foxton at work and befriended him, bringing him a drink after a hard day's hanging.

Calcraft provided an oral history of his life in old age, and told a number of anecdotes about his entering the craft. Foxton told him all about the job, saying it was 'a miserable calling, a wretched, despicable occupation' but that did not deter him. What sums up Calcraft's attitude was his statement to Foxton that he was open to anything that brought something in to support him and his wife. 'You are a rum 'un wanting to take up my line of business' said Foxton. Calcraft was certainly a puzzling character, but he took to the hanging art very well. Luckily for Calcraft, the deputy hangman, who would have taken over the job on Foxton's retirement, was seventy years old. Calcraft put in his letter of application. In general, these documents make fascinating reading, as hangmen throughout history have had all kinds of reasons for wanting to do such an unpleasant line of work. Calcraft wrote, 'Gentlemen, having been informed that the office of executioner will soon be vacant, I beg very humbly to offer myself as a candidate. I am twenty-nine years of age, strong and robust, and have had some experience in the office. I am familiar with the mode of operation, having had, some months ago, been engaged in an emergency to execute two men at Lincoln. I did so, and as the two culprits passed off without a struggle, the execution was performed to the entire satisfaction of the sheriff of the County.'

The hanging in question is interesting. The records show that at Lincoln in 1829 Thomas Lister was hanged for burglary and George Wingfield for highway robbery. The whole business was very irregular. Wingfield's attack was brutal in the extreme, and he was a Lincoln man, so he was not hanged at the Castle, but on a temporary gallows in the lower city, probably as a warning to citizens not to transgress. This was done at the sessions house yard. Lister, who was a huge man over six feet tall and weighing fifteen stones, was hanged on the same day after eating a pound and a half of beefsteak. He was hanged at eleven-thirty and Wingfield at one in the afternoon. There is some confusion as to whether or not Calcraft was there because 1828 was the year given for his work at Lincoln, and there were no hangings that year. He must have officiated then, and the account says that 'the Newgate hangman was sent for'. It seems that the man in question was old Mr Cheshire, who would have succeed Foxton had he not been so aged. The Lincoln executions were on 27 March, and Calcraft was appointed on 4 April, so some record somewhere is wrong, unless Calcraft went with old Cheshire and did more than simple standing by. He may have learned to pinion and to place the hood over the heads at Lincoln. He certainly had the confidence behind that letter of application – the tone of a man who is sure that, having had a 'taster', he could indeed do the work.

There was a competitor – an ex-soldier called Smith – but he had no experience, so that surely swung the decision in Calcraft's favour. Calcraft also had to perform some floggings on taking up the appointment – it was not all ropes and pinions. In the 1820s, whippings were administered for a range of offences and sentences often meant that 24 to 36 lashes were ordered. Again, we have his own words on this. He said that when he arrived in the flogging yard he was 'a little nervous, being afraid I might make some mistake: four young ruffians had to undergo the punishment. The mode of operation had been explained to me by the prison officials and I got through the task in a way that seemed to be altogether satisfactory to those who were present . . .'

Calcraft was beginning to make a lot of money in his job. He was paid for the floggings and the hangings, and also he was a shoemaker, and he was living at the time in Devizes Street, Islington with his wife, Louisa. He soon became the professional hangman who could be called anywhere across the land, and he also kept up his hobbies of fishing and rearing animals. He also loved gardening, and altogether, this image of the countryman who happened to have a steady job as

Another of Calcraft's clients, Elizabeth Fenning.
Author's collection

hangman made all his work part of a comfortable, fulfilling lifestyle. He was even known to walk to a hanging hand in hand with his little daughter. He was keen to acquire his own set of tools for the trade, and he bought his ropes himself.

It was not long before some of the major felons of the age came his way as clients for the drop. He gave a lot of thought to administering quick deaths, such as tugging on legs and jumping on the backs of swinging criminals, fighting to breathe as they were strangled. He even came up with his own gear for improving on pinioning: 'The old pinions used to hurt the fellows so. This waist strap fits every person and is not the least uncomfortable.' This was a special harness he made with a leather belt attached and several buckles. His trade was becoming even more theatrical the more the crowds came to see the deaths. In 1866 black curtains were attached to the scaffold so that there was some element of privacy in what had always been a totally open, public scene of anguish.

Generally, several important personages at the time thought Calcraft to be possessed of that rare professional distance required in such an unsavoury job; he was detached and cold. He had learned to turn off any emotional contact he might have felt with the condemned – and we have to recall that early in his career he was hanging young people and women fairly often. His youngest victim was a nine-year-old boy who had been convicted for arson, though it has to be said that executions of children were very rare. Most were transported up to the 1850s. One journalist said of him: 'He took the business businesslike.' One witness to Calcraft at work wrote: ' . . . the oddest thing of all was to see Calcraft take the pinioned, fin-like hand of the prisoner and shake it, when he had drawn the white cap over the face and arranged the rope.'

One of the strangest episodes in his life was when he himself was in court – being tried for failing to support his mother. Sarah Calcraft, over seventy in 1850, was in the Witham Union Workhouse in Hatfield Peveril. Calcraft found himself standing in the dock at Worship Street Police Court, answering the charges. The overseers had taken proceedings against Calcraft for funding to maintain the old lady. At first, evidence of Calcraft's income was not produced so it was adjourned, but when it convened again, there were witnesses testifying on Calcraft's income. Sarah's story came out in print in *The Times*. She had been in desperate circumstances for some time, living with her daughter. Another son was simply a wastrel, a feckless drifter, and so it fell upon William to take the brunt of the accusations of neglect. Calcraft was ordered to pay three shillings a week, and he claimed that such a sum was beyond his capabilities. Sarah died five years later, after being supported by William.

William Calcraft's name became familiar to the public because of his hanging the villains in some large-scale killings. The Courvoisier case was certainly in that category. Lord William Russell had been found dead on 6 May in his own home; when discovered, the staff found that the room suggested an attack by a burglar who ransacked the place after killing his Lordship. This was something that deeply disturbed Victorian high society – an aristocrat murdered in his own home. The killer was found out by some persistent detective work; a search of his room located a stash of stolen jewels behind a skirting-board. The *Sunday Times* made much of the event: 'The excitement produced in high life by the dreadful event is almost unprecedented, and the feeling of apprehension for personal safety increases every hour, particularly among those of the nobility . . .' So prominent and fascinating was the case that even an attempt on the life of Queen Victoria by a young man called Oxford did not make interest recede. When the case came to court at the Old Bailey, there were three earls, a duke and some higher clergy present. It seemed as though the Swiss butler might not be charged, as everything was circumstantial, but then there was high drama when a woman brought some engraved silver spoons which had been left by Courvoisier at her home not long after the murder. This meant that he would hang.

The butler confessed on the scaffold. There were probably around 40,000 people there to see Calcraft hang Courvoisier on 6 July. Among the crowd were the two great writers Thackeray and Dickens. Dickens was very deeply affected by what he saw, and a few years later he wrote in the *Daily News* about the horrible spectacle: 'It was so loathsome, pitiful and vile a sight, that the law appeared to be as bad as he, or worse; being much the stronger, and shedding around it a far more dismal contagion.'

The actual hanging was described by *The Times* reporter, referring to Calcraft and to the victim: 'During this operation he lifted up his head and raised his hands to his breast. In a moment the hangman drew the fatal bolt, the drop fell and in this attitude the murderer perished without any violent struggle.'

In April, 1849 he had to hang a young woman, Sarah Thomas. Just seventeen and working in Bristol, Sarah was working in service with a hard, cruel woman who used to beat her and deprive her of food. Sarah could take no more and determined to kill her mistress while she slept: she hit her on the head and smashed her skull. She would have to hang, and Calcraft made his way to Bristol to do the job. It was to be a terrible ordeal for him. When he approached her in the condemned cell she cried 'I won't be hanged . . . take me home!' He had to pinion her as she struggled and warders had to help him to restrain her. There was the usual crowd gathered in the yard and the young girl shouted and fought all the way to the noose. He determined to end her life as quickly as possible and did so with real aplomb. Later he said of that case, 'I never felt so much compunction as I did yesterday at Bristol, having to bring that young girl to the scaffold . . . She was, in my opinion, one of the prettiest and most intellectual girls I have met with . . .'

On 28 November that year, James Bloomfield Rush murdered Isaac Jermy and his son Jermy, at Stanfield Hall near Norwich. Rush also attacked and wounded two women. The murders were over his claim to inherit the family estate. The killer waited until the family were having dinner before he made his move, and the story reads like a modern 'spree killing' episode, as Rush appeared wearing a black cloak and wore a mask. He shot the father and son, and also shot Mrs Jermy as she tried to protect her husband. The maid was shot in her thigh. The police soon investigated Rush, as he was the main suspect with a clear motive. He was arrested and stood trial in Norwich. The trial was soon in print, a full account, in small print and with a drawing of Rush prominent. The booksellers got rich, and again, London society took a profound interest in the case.

Norwich castle, where Rush was held and hanged. Pamela Brooks Collection

When it came to the hanging, the regional railway put on special trains for the crowds. The appeal of the drama is not difficult to appreciate: after all, once again, in a home of landed gentry, a slaughter had taken place from within the family – and Mrs Jermy had had to have her arm amputated, following her heroic act in trying to save her husband. Calcraft, as the instrument of the law, both legal and moral, was the public face of proper retribution.

A broadside printed at the time gives minute detail regarding the culprit's last hours: 'The condemned convict Rush was visited on Monday by the whole of his family of nine children . . . Parent and children embraced each other . . . a large number of persons waited outside the castle to witness the departure of the prisoner's family . . .' The rituals of executions were changing from the sheer directness of 'the last dying words' speeches and Newgate biographies to the vicarious pleasures of learning, with morbid fascination, about the felon's last hours, intimately and with a certain degree of sick interest.

The scaffold was outside Norwich gaol. So cool was Rush that, even when hooded and ready for death, he said to the hangman through the material, as the noose was tied,

'Put the noose a little higher, and take your time!' There was a massive crowd watching, and of course Rush had been loudly abused as he walked to the scaffold. Calcraft did the hanging quickly, but of course, Rush took some minutes to die. As usual, death was by strangling.

As is usually evident in any biography of a hangman, there were mistakes, fiascos and failures in Calcraft's career. In 1856, for instance, at Newgate, he had to hang the killer William Bousfield. The condemned man had been desperate to take his own life and to cheat the noose; he had even put his face into the fire in the cell. The man was then carried out to meet his death, but matters were exacerbated by the fact that Calcraft had been sent a threatening letter, saying that he would be killed if he hanged Bousfield. There was the man waiting to hang, sitting in a chair, and the hangman expecting to be shot at any second; Calcraft quickly pulled the lever to release the drop and then ran inside the prison, expecting a bullet. But the victim had grappled with the edge of the platform and had not yet swung when Calcraft was induced to return to the scaffold. Eventually, the man was pushed to his death. His legs had to be held.

We have a few scraps of anecdotes about Calcraft other than the accounts of hangings. Sergeant Ballantyne, for instance, wrote his memoirs in 1882 and wrote: 'It is only right, whilst mentioning the celebrities connected with the Old Bailey, that I should allude to one other personage. Rarely met with upon festive occasions, he was, nevertheless, accustomed to present himself after dinner on the last day of sessions. He was decently dressed, a quiet looking man. Upon his appearance he was presented with a glass of wine. This he drank to the health of his patrons, and expressed with becoming modesty his gratitude for past favours and his hopes for favours to come. He was Mr Calcraft, the hangman.'

Calcraft retired in 1874, just as the genius of the science of hanging, William Marwood, was coming onto the scene. As the doyen of hangman history, Geoffrey Abbotts wrote of Calcraft's demise: 'It is likely that, having lost his wife and now his job, he simply lost heart, for he subsequently became more of a recluse, dying in his home in Poole Street on the evening of Saturday 13 December 1879.'

CHAPTER 7

Samuel Burrows

In 1835, a broadside headed 'The Conversion and Death of Samuel Burrows' was published, and it claims to be an account of the life of the Cheshire hangman, Samuel Burrows, as told in an interview with him the day before he died:19 October 1835. Burrows had died of a 'liver complaint' it recorded. Through the considerable pain, Burrows told the story of his life in that career, spanning twenty-four years, in which time he had executed fifty-three felons. Burrows' place of work had been the gallows in front of the new City Gaol and House of Correction, built in 1807 to replace the old Northgate Gaol at Chester. It is clear from old prints that from the famous city walls, hangings could have been seen, so it is not difficult to imagine the crowds with their grandstand views.

As with so many hangmen, Burrows took a pride in his work and he also had a moral perspective on the nature and purpose of the office. He said in that last conversation that he had had many enemies, but that ' . . . when they rebuked me I laughed at them, for it was all folly, for I solemnly declare I never injured any person in my life . . .' Here, he is making clear the fact that a hangman is performing a public duty – something done without malice. He insisted on his 'innocence' of anything homicidal, as every hangman has to do, perceiving judicial killing as something totally different from a common murder outside the law of the land. The tone of Burrows' statements makes him seem like a well controlled, equable character, someone who weighs and considers words before speaking, a circumspect man, something valuable for this hated profession. So morally upright was the man that he had made sure that his own son was brought to justice for theft. This boy, Charles, was given seven years' transportation and went to the prison ships in the Thames, the hulks, before being shipped across the world to Van Dieman's Land.

Burrows had lost contact with his son, and noted that he would not see him again before his imminent death. Charles was more than likely living a new life abroad and would probably have made a new life for himself after probationary years at the penitentiary, most likely at Port Arthur. Burrows' attitude to all this family tragedy is uncomplaining and accepting. The fact that his son was a wrongdoer did not change anything in his attitudes.

The Cheshire hangman was active in the years when the country

The Dumb Steeple, a Luddite rendezvous.
The author

was in political and economic turmoil. Between c.1810 and 1834 when he was in office, crimes against property were common as the working classes and the underclass such as maimed soldiers and beggars were on the roads; poaching was common, and in the years at the end of his period in office, the 1830s, there was agricultural trouble as well as urban protests and riots, over all kinds of matters, as it was a time of depression and social unrest.

Burrows was brought up in the rural working class; there is no detail about exactly what he did, and what skills he learned. What is certain is that, like Askern and Curry, it was the payment of the work that was most attractive. I say that because he was fond of a drink, and he fits the template of the typical executioner of his time in that, of course. There is no escaping the fact that the common hangman in the Regency years was particularly a person to be reviled and scorned. He was one of the instruments of the repressive authoritarian government, paranoid from the fears of revolution which had happened across the Channel, and worried that anarchy in the streets would grow rapidly as new industries and rural enclosure brought the 'rabble' into towns. It was an age in which the local militias were often called out to stop the riots and protests, and the landlords and wealthier land-proud middle class feared for their lives. Many, like Patrick Bronte in Haworth, kept a pistol and perhaps fired it in practice as he did, in his rural parish, scared that when night fell, he and his daughters would be easy victims of desperate gangs.

In Cheshire in Burrows' time, the common crimes were very much what they were elsewhere in England: machine-braking, riot, destruction of property, murder, highway robbery, arson and infanticide. Burrows was in business against the Luddites, as mentioned earlier in Yorkshire. In 1812 Luddites attacked a mill in Stockport and fifteen men were sentenced to die. However, in keeping with the trend of that time to try to commute sentences where possible, there were just two men waiting for Burrows' dealing out death: John Temple and Joseph Thompson. What was happening in that horrendous year of 1812 was that magistrates across the counties of Yorkshire, Lancashire and Cheshire were trying to communicate with the various county sheriffs to have militia standing by, and also to infiltrate the gangs of Luddites by applying the services of *agents provocateurs* to mix with the enemy and spy on them.

Thompson had been involved with an attack on John Goodair's factory at Edgeley; he and others had started a fire and destroyed the new power-looms that were the focus of hatred and unrest. There was a particular witness who saw him, and she was secure because the rioters left when the militia arrived. Temple was in a gang that did something equally horrific in that context – they broke into a private residence and threatened the family, saying they wanted guns. Temple was arrested and stolen materials were found on him. A double hanging was ordered.

The report of their executions is painfully familiar in the chronicles of hanging: Thompson did the worst thing a hangman could do in those days when the strangulation incurred led to a slow death – he tied the knot at the back by the thick muscle of the neck, not close to the carotid artery. Poor Thompson dangled in agony, fighting for life, doing the 'rope dance' for seven minutes. Temple was more fortunate and died comparatively quickly. But Burrows was not deterred by this error. In fact, local papers make it clear that he tended to swagger and make it clear to his public that he was unmoved by anything. Even after he had hanged his one woman victim – Edith Morrey – it was reported that he was not noticeably affected (as Calcraft was).

The Morrey case was one of those events that put into the public arena the whole matter of petty treason as opposed to murder. This was 1813, a time when the burning of wives for murdering their husbands was not on the statute book, and had that not been the case, the usual custom of strangling the woman before she was at the stake would have been Burrows's job. In 1790 that barbarous penalty was abolished, though there were cases of that abolition being ignored in some places. Luckily and mercifully, she was hanged. Morrey had plotted the murder of her husband, with a man called Lomas actually doing the deed. The judge thought that Lomas was 'the least guilty' and so the wife was seen as the worst criminal in the affair, branded 'the principal in the horrid crime'.

Burrows was very much in demand in 1813; that was the case across the land then, due to all kinds of social antagonism. Most of the offences were very extreme – notably arson and destruction of property. But it was in 1820 that there was a major event in Burrows' career. It was not surprisingly a double hanging that was the cause. But oddly, for it was the kind of stunt that the drunk Curry might have done, his action here goes against his deathbed insistence that he did no wrong to anyone. In fact, what he did was give the already maligned profession an even more bad press. He was due to hang two young men – William Rickington and Ralph Ellis. The former had gone into Coddington rectory by force and stolen materials, then set fire to the building. Ellis, only nineteen, had burgled a home in Ellesmere Port. What Burrows did was reported by the local paper: 'In affixing the ropes, the fellow who fills the disgusting office tried the length of them, by applying with the utmost *sang froid* the noose of one to his own neck; some person in the crowd cried out *For shame, Shame!* The fellow repeated the motion, smiling at his own callosity of feeling, which called forth the execration of the multitude . . .'

As historian Derek Yarwood has pointed out, the local newspapers took against Burrows and made sure that the world knew what a drunkard their public hangman was. Yarwood writes: 'Whereas before the Chester papers had appeared content to protect the anonymity of the city's hangman, the perennial Burrows had the kind of personality and presence they found impossible to ignore . . .' But there was no smoke without fire. Before a hanging in 1826, of a burglar, Burrows was actually kept under lock and key on the night before the execution, merely to keep him away from the drink, under watch at the Governor's house.

This habit of ensuring the hangman's sobriety carried on after that case; in 1829 when he had a double execution to control, he was restrained again, this time in a prison cell. Once more, we have to note that clearly there was no substitute, or surely an obvious difficulty in obtaining an assistant, such was the obloquy placed on the profession.

Although Burrows' reign was generally one in which he was always in disgrace or at least fulfilling the general image of the public hangman as a dissolute, low creature, sub-human and beneath contempt, there was one aspect of his career, related to so-called 'social crime' that shows another side to him, and indeed to the justice system and personnel at the time. 'Social crime' was generally the kind of offence related to the game laws. In a world where the wealthy propertied folk kept a jealous and zealous guard of their goods and game, poaching was seen as a legal issue. This is because men would shoot a rabbit or a hare to feed a hungry family, not simply for the criminal frisson and the sheer trigger-happy pleasure of hunting at night. In 1829, a man called Henshall and his crime demonstrated some of the associated problems.

Henshall was only twenty, a farmer, and he joined a gang going poaching one night, on the land of the Earl of Stamford. The Earl was fighting fire with fire, very much in the manner of the western sheriffs who raised a posse. Henshall and his friends found themselves pitted against a large body of gamekeepers and assorted recruited men, and someone in the young man's gang wounded a gamekeeper. Henshall was caught and charged; in the 1820s there was a universal paranoia against all kinds of rural crime, and the established power-base in both Westminster and in the counties wanted deterrents. Henshall was to die. After the age-old practice of a fellow criminal saving his neck by turning King's evidence, Henshall, it seems, became the 'patsy' of the gang and took the brunt of the punishment.

The subsequent events in court and in gaol were highly irregular. Even the judge, Mr Justice Jervis, a straight-laced man who had earlier written to the Home Secretary, protesting about the 'vile' Sunday papers, wept. In that letter, he had said that the moral backbone of the nation was rotting, and 'violated with a face of brass the constitution and laws of this country'. This same man was now visibly moved by the plight of young Henshall. Contrary to his popular image, so was Burrows. The newspaper report said,

'Even the executioner, hardened as he is by his natural disposition, and his long familiarity with scenes of this nature, even he was moved to tears by the affecting scenes in the ante-room, as well as those whose painful duty it was to witness it . . .' The painful scenes were of Henshall praying and begging divine forgiveness. His behaviour was exactly the kind of thing that the journalists and social critics of the day wanted in their accounts of hangings – repentance and confession.

Burrows was involved in a mishap of proportions that would have made even Curry look proficient. This was in 1834 – a year of living very dangerously in England. At that time, the results of poverty and repression were evident everywhere. A cursory read of *The Times* for that year reflects the sense of danger and violence everywhere, and Chester was no different. Burrows found that he had four men to hang in April 1834. One of these, John Carr, had committed a terribly savage attack on a man, with multiple stabbings, over a few pence. But, as with Curry at York, Burrows was to be troubled by hanging several victims at once. It was an event somewhere on the cusp between horror and dark comedy, because the bolt did not move and Burrows desperately tried to shake and shove the device into action. The four hooded men, awaiting eternity, stood and shuddered. What followed was the hangman's nightmare. All four men went into the air, kicking and fighting for life, and one of them got his feet on the wood supporting the scaffold. The crowd that day had an extra treat in terms of 'turning-off' drama.

At various times, Burrows was attacked by the good citizens of Chester, but he deserved some kind of retribution for his sheer arrogance and drunken displays. On one occasion he had taken too much beer and was publicly disgracing himself by talking about his prowess with the rope, actually holding some clothes of a former dead felon. He was himself in court, facing the judge, after that disgusting performance. He was fined five shillings and if he could not pay that promptly, he would have been arguably the most abused and reviled character in Chester history – a hangman in the stocks. It was certainly not unknown for hangmen to be hanged, but it was virtually impossible for a hangman to be stocked or pilloried, as the event would have totally ruined the man in question. However, Burrows had no good reputation to lose, of course. He paid the fine.

Sam Burrows died in 1835 and after that, Chester hangings were rare affairs, with hangmen being brought in to do the work; William Calcraft was usually the man for the job. Burrows' record is overall nothing to be proud of; he goes into the dark chronicles of hangmen as one of the worst drunks in an occupation notable for its use of 'Dutch courage' in seeing the turning off through to death. Burrows would not only have found beer easily available at any time of day: if he needed extra confidence he could have bought gin. One street-walker of early Victorian London wrote: 'Demands for gin assailed us on all sides, women old and young, girls and boys in the most woeful tatters, some cried for a pint, some for a glass . . .'

Drink, as with almost all the notorious hangmen, had been both the ruin and the cause of success for Burrows. But of course, in his dying words as he spoke of his life, he could say with resignation, 'I know I have many enemies, and when they rebuked me I laughed at them.' At least he survived, unlike poor John Ellis whom we shall meet later, a man who took his own life. As Ellis's biographer, Jack Doughty, wrote, 'As public executioner, he once possessed nerves of steel. Now they

THE
CONVERSION
AND
DEATH
OF
SAMUEL BURROWS.

Samuel Burrows is no more, he ended his career in the 63rd year of his age, at his residence, near Gorse Stacks, Chester, on the 20th October, 1835. It appears according to his testimony while confined to his bed during the last three months, he has been subject to the liver complaint, and was in great pain, which he bore with extreme fortitude, and paid every attention to his religious duties, imploring for mercy to his Redeemer, who desireth not the death of a sinner. He experienced his kindness to the unfortunate individuals 53 in number when on the scaffold in different places; he could not refrain trusting in his mercy, and we are happy to announce that the Bible and Prayer-book were his constant study, and gave up all worldly thoughts, and when he became unable to read, he was thankful to any person who rendered him scriptural advice, last week he was visited by the Rev. W. Clarke, of little St. John's, the excellent discourses from different passages of the scriptures took the the greatest impression on his mind, and he joined in prayer during the whole of the ceremony. On Monday he said I know I have many enemies and when they rebuked me I laughed at them, for it was all folly, for I solemnly declare I never injured any person in my life but was always willing to advise them for their reformation, who were straying from the paths of innocence and virtue, I never sent a poor person from my door, without relieving, which is well known to them that applied in such cases, which I trust will be before me in heaven, I am innocent of every thing alledged to my charge respecting the unfortunate creatures, for they made their peace with me either before or on the drop, considering themselves no longer creatures of this world, it was well known the sentence of the law must take its course. He said many is desirous of taking the job, but thank God I am done, he then turned on his back in the bed, and lifting up his hands to heaven, he repeated the Lord's Prayer, and in conclusion with an audable voice for thine is the kingdom, the power and the glory, for ever and ever, Amen; exclaiming I die in peace with all mankind. On being questioned respecting his son Charles, he said he was a bad lad, and would not keep from evil company he might be here to see the last of me, but he volunteered to go abroad from the Hulks, and if he remained he would get off for about four years, for all that was against him was stealing a pair of stockings, but I was the means of sending him off, for I could not screen such evils, for it would be the greatest injustice to mankind.

Henry, his eldest son enlisted in Lord Combermere's Troops and died in the East Indies. Mary, the wife of Samuel died last March, of a decline, and he has made an assignment of his effects in the club, being 35 years a member, to his nephew. He was born at Ravensm Moor, in the parish of Acton, near Nantwich, in this county, 28th June, 1772. He was 24 years in office, and executed 53 individuals.

Printed for W. Byrne, No. 169, Handbridge, Chester.

had gone to pieces. For over two years he had suffered from neuritis, heart trouble and nervous trouble . . .' Those words could apply equally well to Samuel Burrows. We have to remember that in his time, hangings were barbaric, with no consideration given to the anatomical factors and to humane death. In the years before the mid-Victorian years, the range of capital offences was horrendously large. In Scotland, a young man called Aikenhead was hanged for blasphemy in 1697, Bible in hand, although he had offended by saying that Christianity was a 'load of nonsense'.

Any number of such victims, for offences ranging from theft to poaching and from assault to robbery, came Burrows's way, and he had to find a way to cope with all that brutal 'turning off' of desperate, poor and deprived lives: some were evil villains and others he executed were feckless and half-starved. Such was the lot of the common hangman.

CHAPTER 8

The Long-Drop Man

Before William Marwood from Horncastle, Lincolnshire, emerged in the 1870s as a hangman who was to exhibit a whole new attitude to the profession, there was a considerable movement for reform and abolition of the death penalty. The Consolidation Act of 1861 abolished capital punishment for all offences except treason, murder, piracy with violence and arson in dockyards. In the mid-Victorian years there were fewer hangings, and notably in 1854 there were only five hangings; there was a groundswell of opinion that hanging should be abolished. In 1864 there was a debate in the House of Commons and a Royal Commission was established to look into the matter. There had been a previous enquiry held in 1856, specifically looking at public executions, reporting on 'the present mode of carrying into effect capital punishments, chaired by the Bishop of Oxford.

William Marwood.
Laura Carter

The sixth Duke of Richmond was the chairman, a Tory, and he had such men as Gathorne Hardy and Lord Stanley on the Commission with him. Their recommendations were that there should be two divisions of murder, 'degrees' – and that first degree murder should have the death penalty. They also thought that the tricky subject of infanticide should be understood separately from murder, that judges should be given the power of the sentence again, and that public executions should be ended. Some members of the group, including the famous speaker John Bright, wanted the death penalty abolished. A long debate on the 'two degrees' followed and in the end, it was decided that a better distinction was the murder/ manslaughter one. The definition of murder was that the aggressor clearly had an intention to take the life of another, or to do grievous bodily harm 'dangerous to life'. Spencer Walpole in the Conservative government, tried to institute five varieties of homicide, all versions of murder, but that failed to materialise. Homicide Amendment Bills in 1872 and 1874 were attempted and even by 1878 the bill failed to bring about radical reform. But at least public executions stopped, in 1868.

William Marwood stepped in as principal hangman at this time, taking up his first work in 1872, and hanging 167 criminals between that year and 1883. Marwood was to become legendary in popular culture and a quip about him was circulated: 'If Pa killed Ma, who would kill Pa? Marwood.' He was a shoemaker by trade, and in his shop he used a trapdoor in his warehouse hoist on Wharf Road, Horncastle, to perfect what would be his long drop method, a more humane way of helping a felon into the next world. Marwood realised that the normal method of hanging was brutal, in that the rope was tied haphazardly at the neck, and so death was by slow strangulation.

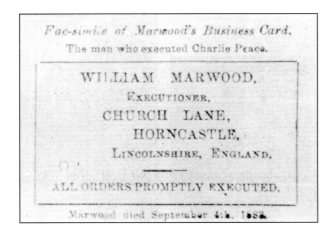

Marwood's business card.
Author's collection

Cobb Hall, Lincoln Castle, the hanging place. The author

He saw that a longer drop, in relation to the weight of the victim, together with a knot tied at the main artery, would make for a speedy end.

In 1879 he was interviewed by a writer from the *Lincoln Gazette*; he was described as having a hard face, 'shrewd' but not unkindly'. The interviewer provided a fuller account:

> (his face) was strongly marked, rugged almost in its deep lines and furrows. The eyes were quiet, resolute and penetrating; the mouth shut firm and tight as one of his own nooses . . . What struck me most were his hands — knotted, twisted, vigorous hands, the hands of a man who had worked with them for years at some severe manual labour and who could use them with Herculean strength and tenacity if required.

Marwood told the journalist that hanging was 'All as stops murder.' He argued that fear of the rope 'kept a man's blood down and his temper cool' and he said that hanging killers was 'Only another way of controlling vermin — vermin have a mortal sting and as such should be put out of the way of doing harm . . .'

He was not at all bothered by the reputation his trade had for the

Gallows at York shown in Calcraft's time. Author's collection

public. In fact, he agreed to sit for his effigy at Madame Tussaud's establishment and John Theodore Tussaud remembered him well, recalling that Marwood used to go to the studios when he was feeling melancholy, drink some gin and smoke a pipe. Then he would walk around the chambers, enjoying the thrill of seeing the waxworks of some of the people he had executed. Tussaud wrote, 'He had no objection to his own effigy being in their company . . . Usually he was accompanied by his old dog, a grizzled terrier that had played with his ropes and caught rats in his master's business bags. On one occasion he was at the chambers, feeling down, and talked about his dog dying. Someone listening thought it was fun to ask Marwood if he should not hang the dying creature, and the hangman replied, 'No, hang a man, but my dear old dog, never!'

Marwood took his business very seriously and he was much in demand. A letter to his wife Ellen gives a clear impression of his lifestyle, printed here with his spelling:

Dear Ellen,

This is to say that I sent a letter on thousday last on my arrival at Clonmal in Ireland t say that I was all well – now this is to say that I left dublin last night about 9 a clock for Hollehead arrived about 3 a clock this

For Birmingham arrived about 11 a clock to Day I ham now in Birmingham With the governor waiting to see the governor of Bristol at

*half past towTo Day and then I leave here for Cambridge. This after-
noon all well so ifAll well I shall return on Monday night or Tuesday
morning I hope all is wellAt home tell my poor boy nero that is marster
is coming home, remember meTo Mrs Moodey I hope she will call on
Sunday to take tea now take good . . . ofMy poor nero be good to polley
I hope I shall find all things bright on my Return . . .*

His spelling was clearly not as good as Calcraft's, who was always a
capable scholar. But this does indicate the sheer intensity and rush of
his professional life, being that of a travelling expert, reliable and
proficient. We also have an idea of his payment, as this letter from
the sheriff of Galway notes in 1882: 'There are a number of executions here on Friday the 15th December next, and I wish to be
informed if you will be able to carry them out on the day named,
and also your charge for same. As it is always one day's job, I
presume your charge will be the same as last time, £20 for the day.'
The sheriff, Mr Midlington, made it clear that the costs incurred
came out of his own pocket, perhaps hinting that he did not expect a
rise in the charge.

Marwood was destined to officiate at some notable and often in-
famously political hangings. His trip to Galway in response to the
above request was one of the most sensational trials and executions in
nineteenth-century Ireland. Known as the Maamtrasna murders, the
brutal events meant that three men were to be hanged: Patrick and
Myles Joyce and Patrick Casey. What happened was that Marwood
found himself being accused of making a mess of things. The *Western
Mail* explained the furore:

> *After hanging an hour the bodies were taken down, and Mr Collingham
> held an inquest. After formal evidence had been given, Dr Rice was
> examined and deposed: "I am surgeon at Galway gaol, and have
> examined the bodies of the three men executed this morning. Patrick
> Casey died of a fracture of the cervical spine, and death in this case must
> have been nearly instant . . . Patrick Joyce had exactly the same injuries
> . . . Myles Joyce died from strangulation, no fracture of the neck bones
> having taken place at all. I consider that death took place over one to two
> minutes . . .*

The Galway officials were displeased, and the jurors said that they
wanted Marwood there to give an explanation. It was said that
Marwood was at fault because, as Myles Joyce was 'not so passive as
the other two' the hangman should have tied his knot first.

This was a familiar incident in nineteenth-century hanging. Even
the best hangman made mistakes, and it was at multiple hangings that

they were most likely to happen. In this case (and it was a rare thing) Marwood's response was printed. The hangman said, 'Myles Joyce had in some way got his hand entangled in the rope and he had been trying to push it down. Death was instantaneous, as there was nothing wrong with the rope, I have used it before at Limerick, York Castle, Bodmin, Cornwall and Worcester . . . I gave all the men an equal drop of nine feet . . .'

His most celebrated hanging was surely the execution of the famous Phoenix Park murderers in 1882. A gang had murdered the Chief Secretary for Ireland, Lord Frederick Cavendish, and his under-secretary, in broad daylight in Phoenix Park, Dublin, while the victims were walking in the park. Four men had leapt from a cab and stabbed him to death. The 'Irish Invincibles' as they called themselves, sent black-bordered cards to the Dublin papers. Joseph Brady had gone with one group and Daniel Curley with another, after a planning meeting at *Wrenn's Tavern* near Dublin Castle. They agreed to split up and decide on where the attack should take place. They had made sure that they had correctly identified Harry Burke, the under secretary, so there would be no mistakes. As they were gathering in the park, there was almost a very big problem for them because a police superintendent called Mallon was going to the park to meet one of his contacts and he met a plain-clothes detective who warned him of at attempt on his life; Mallon left, so the coast was clear for the assassins.

Another turn of fate for the victims was that Cavendish had been offered a ride instead, but had insisted that he walk with Burke. As Cavendish was only just in place as the Secretary there were things to talk through, and a stroll seemed a pleasant way to do that. But they were walking to an appointment with death. After a man called Timothy Kelly had advanced and knifed Cavendish, the gang were soon upon them, with Brady cutting Burke's throat in the assault. They made their escape, hoping to drive around the city and approach Dublin from another entrance, thus making a platform for some kind of alibi, but a detective had seen a number of them and would later identify them. The first move in apprehending the gang came when a driver broke down and told the tale. It was not long before they were tried and sentenced and William Marwood was crossing the Irish Sea with his ropes and pinion.

Sixteen of the Invincibles were tried and five were hanged; James Carey turned state's evidence. Joseph Brady was executed on 14 May, sentenced to death by Mr Justice O'Brien, and others followed, Marwood hanging them at Kilmainham gaol. The events went down in popular history, as in the song *Monto* recorded by The Dubliners, in which we have the rhyme:

When Carey told on Skin-the-goat
O'Donnell caught him on the boat
He wished he'd never been afloat the filthy skite,
'Twasn't very sensible
To tell on the Invincibles
They stood up for their principles, day and night..

Marwood's other outstanding cases were the execution of master criminal Charles Peace and of Kate Webster, the latter being one of the hangman's more efficient jobs. Kate was born in Ireland but settled in London. In 1879 she worked in Richmond, as housemaid to a Mrs Julia Thomas. Kate liked a late-night drink and loud company, and her employer was very strict, tending to reprimand her too often and a level of antagonism developed which escalated into something very savage. Kate Webster, in a torrid temper, went for an axe and then sliced into Mrs Thomas's head with the blade.

Kate Webster then cut up her employer's corpse. She tried to boil away the remains, and she had a tough time scrubbing the walls clean of blood because hacking with an axe is very messy. Her plan was to take bits of the body out in bags, a few pieces at a time, and throw them into the Thames. Then, as she realised that she could steal the identity of the lady, she did so and tried to sell the house. Dumping bodies is often the flaw in a killer's designs and so it was with Kate. A fisherman found some of the sacks and reported that to the police. They were soon on Webster's trail.

She was back home in Killane, Ireland, when the officers of the Royal Irish Constabulary arrived to arrest her. Then she was found to have some of the stolen valuables at her home; Webster was brought back to stand trial at the Old Bailey, and was sentenced to death. There was a story in circulation that she had made human dripping from some of the body parts after slicing them, but that was surely an urban myth. The only mystery at the end of the case was the whereabouts of Mrs Thomas's head. She protested her innocence and even on the day of her execution, she caused problems for Marwood, shouting and insulting him and the whole legal process. But this time Marwood was on top form, doing his calculations accurately and ensuring a swift end to her life.

The Victorian public believed, on the whole, with Shakespeare's line, 'Where the offence is great, let the greatest axe fall.' When it came to the case of Charles Peace, there was very little clamour to spare his life. He had become the most notorious villain in Britain up to the advent of Jack the Ripper. Every aspect of his story suggests legend, folk tale, and an element of the grotesque. But he was undoubtedly a

Charles Peace, the Master Criminal, cover for an old local chapbook. The author

candidate for the Holmesian title, 'Master Criminal' as everything about his life was unusual. He was born in 1832, the son of a one-legged lion-tamer, John Peace, and by the age of twelve he was working in a rolling mill at Sheffield, called Millsands. It was a fearful accident at this mill, when a red-hot bar impaled him in the leg, that led to the first stage of his fearsome and ill-formed appearance in later life.

But Peace earned a living, after coming through this, playing the violin and starting a career of petty crime. Ayer writing in 1906 noted, 'He learned to play the violin and learned so quickly that after his recovery he was in demand at concerts . . . On one occasion he had an engagement at a theatre and was billed as 'The Modern Paganini.' His performance consisted of playing on a single string. Unfortunately, his name is linked more with his most notorious murder, at Banner Cross in Sheffield. In 1876 he was in Manchester and he killed a policeman there. Another man, William Habron, was tried and convicted for this, and Peace attended the trial, later saying he had enjoyed the spectacle.

But he began to harass and trail a Mrs Katherine Dyson, the wife of an engineer Peace had got to know. He became such a threatening nuisance that the Dysons moved house, but Peace followed them, and one night as Katherine went to an outside toilet, Peace was there, and he had a gun. When Mr Dyson came out, he was shot. Peace said, 'I'm here to annoy you, and I'll annoy you wherever you go.' He shot Dyson in the head.

Peace then moved to London and began a new life, living as a Mr John Ward. He put up a front of living as an amateur businessman and inventor, but at night he was still doing robberies and burglaries. As he always had a gun on him when at work, he shot and wounded a police officer one night while being chased after a robbery. It was when his mistress, Susan Ward, informed on him that the law finally caught up with the man who did the Banner Cross murder.

Then, in grand comic-strip tradition, Peace tried his most daring escape. He was being escorted to Leeds to stand trial for the Yorkshire murder, and he asked permission, while on the train, to urinate. The escape meant he had to throw himself out of an open carriage window while his handcuffs were momentarily taken off. He dived out but the attempt failed; he was stuck fast and attempted to kick free and hung from the window before falling and seriously injuring himself. He was recaptured and then sent to answer the murder charge in the dock at Leeds. Peace was proved to be the man who killed Arthur Dyson and was sentenced to hang. He may have been responsible for more murders than those at Banner Cross and at Whalley Edge, Manchester.

Marwood hanged Peace on 25 February 1879. The papers were

Armley gaol, where Peace was hanged.
Laura Carter

still full of the stunning achievement of the soldiers at Rorke's Drift during the Zulu War, but Peace's death made the headlines and the front page of the *Police News* which showed Marwood performing the execution and featured a drawing of Marwood's face which is one of the clearest images we have apart from the Tussaud effigy. To the very end, Peace was a 'character'. He joked, 'I wonder if the hangman can cure my sore throat!' Being a man with a sense of drama, he insisted on a last speech, for the sake of the reporters. He said, 'Say my last wishes and my last respects are to my children and their dear mother. I hope that no person will disgrace himself by taunting or jeering them . . . Oh My Lord have mercy on me!'

As for Marwood, cool as always, he said simply, 'He was such a desperate man, but bless you dear Sir, he passed away like a summer's eve.' But Peace will always be remembered as one of Yorkshire's most successful thieves and rogues. Teignmouth Shore once described him: 'Slight as was his frame, his strength was enormous' and there were tales about his habits and rackets, such as this, described by Shore in the same memoir:

Further light upon this really amazing fellow is provided by Sir William Clegg; I quote from one of his letters . . . " a small, spare man, clean shaven and with a very prominent chin, which he could so distort as to make himself almost unrecognisable. Whilst he was in custody . . . he informed me that on many occasions he went to Scotland Yard for the purpose of reading the notice offering the reward for his own apprehension, but that by manipulating his jaw he could escape detection . . .

Marwood's public profile was raised considerably by his connection with such notable cases, of course, and hanging itself was in the news. One bizarre footnote to this was the advent of 'amateur hanging'. In *The Times* under that heading was this intriguing note: 'It has often been remarked that in this country a public execution is generally followed closely by instances of death by hanging, either suicidal or accidental, in consequence of the powerful effect which the execution of a noted criminal produces upon a morbid and unmatured mind.' After an execution in 1850, a Sheffield lunatic hanged himself, and the *Morning Advertiser* of 1849 noted that after the execution of Sarah Thomas in that year there was an amateur hanging death of a man called Yardley, a parricide, by hanging and a family massacre in which a man killed his children, and with the use of a rope. The whole topic was similar to the recent debates on the negative influences of video nasties; one thing is certain – the high profile media attention given to killers such as Peace and Webster did produce images of the hanging ritual in the public mind.

William Marwood's life was eventful and sometimes mysterious, too. After the Phoenix Park hangings he was sent a threatening letter saying he would be assassinated. But his life went on, doing his

The Castle Hill Club, Lincoln. Marwood stayed in the attic.
The author

unpleasant work from town to town. In his own home city of Lincoln he was in the habit of staying in an attic room of what is now the club to the left of the entrance to Lincoln Castle. He was fond of a pint and a pipe and quietly went on with his business.

Marwood's cases in Lincoln were less sensational, and if we look at the hanging of Peter Blanchard on 9 August 1875 for instance, we have a glimpse of the more everyday jobs for the hangman with the long drop. Blanchard was a tanner from Louth, just twenty-six when he became jealous of Louisa Hodgson, his fiancée. She was friendly with a farmer called Campion and Blanchard didn't like it. He took a knife and waited until Campion came out of chapel, but instead of going for him, he later turned his ire on Lousia, stabbing her in her own kitchen. When told that the woman was dead, Blanchard simply said, 'I'm damned glad!' Marwood hanged Blanchard at the Castle, on Cobb Hall, on a rainy day when a large crowd had gathered. There was a thunderstorm as he body fell and the legs jerked. The black flag was raised over Lincoln that day, and the townsfolk knew that William Marwood had been coldly efficient yet again, in ridding the place of its 'vermin'.

Marwood tended to invest his money, but lost most of it unwisely. At his death he was penniless, dying after a fall at a pub while in his cups; and some said that he had been poisoned by the Fenians in revenge for the Invincible hangings. It was 4 September 1883. He was buried in an unmarked grave in the churchyard at Horncastle.

CHAPTER 9

James Berry

James Berry was a man who came to his vocation as hangman after a long list of failures and dead ends in his search for a career which would satisfy him. After a rough and eventful childhood in which he narrowly escaped death or serious injury on a number of occasions, he began to take note of the work being done by Marwood in his fairly short but import reign as public executioner. Marwood, as already briefly mentioned, laboured hard to refine the art of hanging, with attention paid in more detail to the weight of the body and the length of the drop down the trapdoor. The process generally demanded a swiftly handled sequence of actions following the movements of putting on the cap, placing the noose, removing the pin in the lever-frame, pulling the lever and finally making sure the trap and drop worked.

Berry, as he noted in his letter of application after Marwood's death, made a point of stressing that he had actually met and taken advice from the Lincolnshire shoemaker. Marwood had become infamous:

James Berry.
Author's collection

the rhyme, 'If pa killed ma, who would kill pa? Marwood.' This was in common currency and he had been immortalised at Madame Tussaud's waxworks. Berry had paid attention to the skills involved in the work, and it seems that although money was not the major consideration, it was very important to him at the time because he had a wife and family to house and feed. Berry had served in the Bradford police and so had some knowledge of the criminal world and of the nature of urban crime, violent or otherwise. But he soon realised how different and of course, how unique the craft of executing felons actually was in practice.

It was Binns' failure that opened up the work to him; he had been pipped at the post when Binns was first employed, being second in a very long list of applicants. In fact, one of Berry's abiding faults was a bold egoism and lust for publicity as well as respect, and that very nearly cost him the career he sought. He told the press that he had the post before it was really secured. But it appears that the selection panel were so impressed with his profile and past initiative, as well as in his long-standing interest in the work, that they appointed him gladly.

Of course, any of the figures in authority would have soon been aware, had they looked back on the previous hangmen in the century, that there was a likelihood of embarrassment and shame attached to the post, largely as a result of the tendency for the incumbents of the profession to take to drink and to suffer from what we would now call work-related stress. But something about Berry's manner and air of confidence brought him into favour.

James Berry was born in February 1852, at Heckmondwike, where his father, Daniel, was a wool-stapler. He had a hard time at school and his nature contained a strong streak of rebellion which led him to try to run away to sea, play truant and get into all kinds of scrapes. But his police service apparently caused a significant change in him, primarily in his self-regard and confidence. He wrote in his memoirs with an arrogance and vanity about his successes there (and later in the Nottingham police for a short while) with outstanding claims. His achievements read like a Sherlock Holmes of Yorkshire. But both in Bradford and in Nottingham he was restless and demanding, and his personality was abrasive and combative, leading ultimately to resignation.

He had been considering the appeal of the welcome income of the hangman's trade for some time; his range of employment had brought continual frustration and some real financial hardship. But certainly in the case of execution work, he had taken it seriously for some time. When his memoirs were first published, serialised in the *Saturday Post* magazine in 1914, he explained the source of his aims to work as hangman in this way, after he heard newsboys shouting out the news that Marwood had died:

SCALE SHOWING THE STRIKING FORCE OF FALLING BODIES AT DIFFERENT DISTANCES.

Distance Falling in Feet	8 Stone			9 Stone			10 Stone			11 Stone			12 Stone			13 Stone			14 Stone			15 Stone			16 Stone			17 Stone			18 Stone			19 Stone		
Zero	Cw.	Qr.	lb.	Cw.	Qr.	lb.	Cw.	Qr.	lb.	Cw.	Qr.	lb.	Cw.	Qr.	lb.	Cw.	Qr.	lb.	Cw.	Qr.	lb.	Cw.	Qr.	lb.	Cw.	Qr.	lb.	Cw.	Qr.	lb.	Cw.	Qr.	lb.	Cw.	Qr.	lb.
1 Ft.	8	0	0	9	0	0	10	0	0	11	0	0	12	0	0	13	0	0	14	0	0	15	0	0	16	0	0	17	0	0	18	0	0	19	0	0
2 „	11	1	15	12	2	23	14	0	14	15	2	4	16	3	22	18	1	12	19	3	2	21	0	21	22	2	11	24	0	1	25	1	19	26	3	9
3 „	13	3	16	15	2	15	17	1	14	19	0	12	20	3	11	22	2	9	24	1	8	26	0	7	27	3	5	29	2	4	31	1	2	33	0	1
4 „	16	0	0	18	0	0	20	0	0	22	0	0	24	0	0	26	0	0	28	0	0	30	0	0	32	0	0	34	0	0	36	0	0	40	0	0
5 „	17	2	11	19	3	5	22	0	0	24	0	22	26	1	16	28	2	11	30	3	5	33	0	0	35	0	22	37	0	16	39	2	11	41	3	15
6 „	19	2	11	22	0	5	24	2	0	26	3	22	29	1	16	31	3	11	34	1	5	36	3	0	39	0	22	41	2	16	44	0	11	46	2	5
7 „	21	0	22	23	3	11	26	2	0	29	0	16	31	3	5	34	1	22	37	0	11	39	3	0	42	1	16	45	0	5	47	2	22	50	1	11
8 „	22	2	22	25	2	4	28	1	14	31	0	23	34	0	5	36	3	15	39	2	25	42	2	7	45	1	16	48	0	26	51	0	8	53	3	18
9 „	24	0	11	27	0	12	30	0	14	33	0	23	36	0	16	39	0	18	42	0	19	45	0	21	48	0	22	51	0	23	54	0	25	57	0	26
10 „	25	1	5	28	1	23	31	2	14	34	3	4	37	3	22	41	0	12	44	1	2	47	1	21	50	2	11	53	3	1	56	3	19	60	0	9

From this table of the striking force of falling bodies of various weights, falling through different distances, Berry calculated the 'drop' required on the basis that the striking force required was 24cwt.

Berry's table of drops. Author's collection

It almost seemed as if fate had kept me poor to drive me into the position. It seemed that I was predestined from birth to become the follower of Marwood, for, extraordinary though it may seem, the Chief Constable of Bradford was setting out to ask me to take the job at the very moment I was setting out to ask him to use his influence with the people of London.

We have to speculate what character traits in Berry had impressed themselves on the Chief Constable, James Withers. It is very difficult to ascertain exactly what qualities would lead someone to see the potential of 'public hangman' in a person. A profile, taking in the men who have filled that role in British history, would have to include features including religious calling, odd altruistic need to participate in Mosaic justice, and of course, the appeal of cash or freedom in the tradition of felons turned executioners, particularly in Yorkshire. In Berry's case, financial reward was part of it, but the superiors in the police force and perhaps also Marwood (they did meet) saw something else.

Arguably the best way to locate this elusive quality is to observe how he acquired his professionalism and that is closely recorded in the events around his very first job, in Edinburgh in March 1884. We would expect a man to recall such an experience in great detail, and such was the case. The victims in question were two poachers,

William Innes and Robert Vickers. There was still a common feeling around that poaching was a social crime, and that gamekeepers were very much reproached for their work. Some thought that the two men would have a reprieve. But it was not to be, and the account of Berry's weekend there, as retold by Stewart Evans in his recent biography of Berry, makes it clear that the Bradford man was extremely impressive, and as one would expect, he had to go through the hellish torment of that first ordeal, knowing he was taking two young lives, judicially sanctioned or not, still a kind of homicide.

Berry, with his mysterious assistant with a pseudonym of 'Richard Chester', gives an account of the whole period, from arrival on the Thursday to departure after the job was done. He certainly did his homework, doing all kinds of tests on the gallows such as using bags of cement as the body-weights and of course, calculating the drop

From the Life of James Murphy.
Author's collection

required. His religious faith played a part, as he asked for guidance from the Almighty, but also the professionalism in him came through, seen clearly in the way his mental strength held strong against all the emotional and sympathetic thoughts that assailed him as he had to spend many long hours inside the grounds, thinking of the enormity of what he was about to do.

As Stewart Evans describes, the hanging itself was notably efficient and it pleased the officials from the prison and other medical men – a rare achievement in this trade. Berry wrote, 'Everything was done as quick as lightning, and both culprits paid the highest penalty of the law . . .' As Evans also points out (and this is a real mystery), Berry departed from Marwood's practice in one very significant way, and that was in respect of where the knot was placed on the neck. Marwood's belief, later supported by a group of surgeons, was that the knot should be fastened submentally, that is, under the chin and on the left. Berry made his knot under the left ear. That would almost certainly not be as rapid and efficient as a knot over the major artery under the left front of the chin; it would make more of a forceful jolt, affecting the spinal column differently also.

Berry only did one hanging in Yorkshire, but it was a sensational case: that of the Barnsley murderer (again, a poacher) James Murphy. He was a Dodsworth collier who had experienced the urgings of a personal vendetta against a constable called Austwick. Ever since Austwick had arrested him for drunkenness, Murphy had had a burning hatred against the officer. He later went out, with a clear intention of killing Austwick and did so, then after a few days on the run he was tracked down and arrested.

Surely the most remarkable aspect of the Murphy case was his nonchalance and fortitude in the face of the scaffold. Berry has left a detailed account of the conversation he had with the killer, on entering the cell as Murphy was chewing a mutton chop, fully aware that his death was only a few hours away. At the end of the talk, Murphy made a joke. Berry asked, 'I hope you won't give me any trouble when the time comes,' and this followed:

He looked at me and smiled.
'I won't give you any trouble. I am not afraid to die. A lot of people have been making a fuss over this business, and I'm hanged if I can see what there is to make a fuss about.'
I was so surprised at his joke, that I could say nothing, and so I left him and did not see him again until I went to pinion him.

In Berry's career as hangman, he had the especially painful duty of executing five women. One of these, the case of Mary Lefley in

Lincoln Assizes. The author

Lincolnshire, provides one of the most heart-rending and contentious hangings in the entire record of British capital punishment.

In the Lincolnshire village of Wrangle, Mary Lefley, aged forty-nine, lived with her cottager husband, William, ten years her senior. They were living in a freehold property and seemed reasonably happy as far as anyone was aware. On 6 February 1884 various friends called at their cottage and everything seemed normal. Mary set off for Boston to sell produce, and later in the day, around three in the afternoon, William arrived at the home of the local medical man, Dr Bubb. Lefley was extremely ill and the doctor was not there. He staggered in and hit the floor, retching and moaning. He had brought a bowl of rice pudding and told some women present that it had poisoned food in it.

When he was told again that Dr Bubb was not at home, he said, 'That won't do. I want to see him in one minute, I'm dying fast.' A Dr Faskally (the locum) then came and examined him; it was a desperate situation, yet for some reason the doctor had Lefley carried to his own house, where he died.

When Mary came home that evening her behaviour was confused and to some, irrational, which was to have repercussions later on. She actually stated to the doctor that she expected Lefley to claim that he had been poisoned. What was then reported about her is strange indeed. A neighbour who was trying to help made her some tea and Mary said, 'I've had nothing all day because I felt so queer.' Then she talked about making the pudding. 'He told me not to make any pudding as there was plenty cooked, but I said I always make pudding and would do so as usual.' In themselves, these two statements are quite innocuous, but in the context of the later trial they were to prove lethal to her.

At Lincoln Assizes in May 1884 she was in the box; there was no other suspect. The police were convinced that there had been foul play and she was the only suspect. She had been charged on circumstantial evidence only and she pleaded not guilty. But then she had to listen to an astounding piece of evidence from the post-mortem. There had been a massive amount of arsenic in the rice pudding: 135 grains. A fatal dose needs only to be two grains. Despite the fact that some white powder found in her home was found to be harmless, witnesses were called and the trial proceeded. The strongest testimony came from William's nephew, William Lister, who recounted an argument between the couple when his uncle had taken a great quantity of ale. William came to his nephew's bed and told him that he had just attempted suicide.

Other witnesses said that they had heard Mary say that she wished

A typical Victorian depiction of a female killer – Mrs Manning. Author's collection

her husband was 'dead and out of the way'. It was a tough challenge for the defence, and they failed. Mary was sentenced to death and her reply was, 'I'm not guilty and I never poisoned anyone in my life.'

There is a great deal of detail on Berry's account of the horrendous experience of carrying out her execution. Berry, new to the job and anxious to do things right, was of the opinion that he was going to hang an innocent woman. But he was a professional with a task ahead of him and he carried on. He wrote his own account of the process in his memoirs:

> *To the very last she protested her innocence, though the night before she was very restless and constantly exclaimed, "Lord, thou knowest all!"*
> *She would have no breakfast and when I approached her she was in a nervous agitated state, praying to God for salvation . . . but as an innocent woman . . . she had to be led to the scaffold by two female warders.*

Berry records that Mary was ill when he went to fetch her on that fateful morning. She also shouted 'Murder!' Berry wrote with feeling and some repugnance about the whole business, and at having to pinion her. Her cries were piercing as she was dragged along to the scaffold. As Berry reported, 'Our eyes were downcast, our senses numbed, and down the cheeks of some the tears were rolling.' After all, as soon as Berry had arrived at the gaol, a woman warder had said to him, 'Oh Mr Berry, I am sure as can be that she never committed the dreadful crime. You have only to talk to the woman to know that . . .' Berry noted that he 'found the gaol in a state of panic' when he arrived. He recalled that the chaplain's prayers had sounded 'more like a sob' on the last morning of Mary Lefley's life.

The final irony is that, if we believe Berry, that a farmer, who had been humiliated in a deal with Lefley, confessed to the poisoning on his deathbed. He said he had crept into the cottage on that day and put the poison in the pudding.

Berry had always been the kind of man who, when he eventually found his vocation, would revel in it, enjoy it to the full in terms of both inner satisfaction and in his need for acclamation and self-advertisement. Earlier in his life he had made the most of the smallest achievements, showing his ability as a 'spin-doctor' of his own status and reputation. He even had a business card produced, with delicate leaves across the card, his name beneath and his address of '1, Bilton Place, Bradford' also. The card proclaims his profession as well as his name and address: 'James Berry: Executioner' as if it were as ordinary a trade as a blacksmith or a printer at the time. But his life after his hangman years reveal a very different inner personality, more complex than one would have inferred from his public life and opinions.

Berry managed to indulge in all kinds of hobbies and part-time jobs when his career ended. He had various items as souvenirs and some of these were sold to Madame Tussaud's. He also began to take part in lecture tours, as there was always a morbid interest in the general public in the subject of execution. He moved to different addresses in the Bradford area, and he still had his wife, mother-in-law and one of his sons living with him at the time of the 1901 census. It is at this time that we begin to discern some of those deeper qualities explained at length in a vignette of him by his editor, Snowden Ward, who wrote that 'His character is a curious study – a mixture of very strong and very weak traits such as is seldom found in one person.' Ward also noted something that also applied to Albert Pierrepoint later: that his wife knew little of her husband's professional activities. She said that she had lived with him for nineteen years but that she still did not really know him.

Berry had always been a man who looked to any kind of legal activity for earning a few pounds, and that habit was still with him when he was described as 'commission agent, late public executioner.' But his media career was a failure and he took to trading for small profits in retail. What began to emerge then was the drinking habit, something that became more serious as time went on. He once expressed this frankly and simply: 'I knew that it was drink that was the main support of the gallows.' What happened then is that he wrote begging letters to prison authorities and to people in high places in the prison establishment, asking for his job back. But things had moved on and the general attitude was that there was no point in employing a man who had 'given them trouble.' And there were younger men coming through.

Surely one of the most dramatic and compelling stories of this complex man's life is the account of his reclamation, spiritually, after walking out of his home one day with the intention of taking his own life. He wrote in his memoirs, 'I could not have thought it possible that mortal man could become so low and depraved . . . My burning conscience accused me of having wronged my family – my innocent, good and virtuous wife, and my sorely suffering children –with my carryings on in sin and wickedness. There was nothing else for it – I must put an end to my life.'

What happened was that, as he sat on a railway platform, intending to throw himself from the window of a train in a tunnel between Leeds and Bradford, he began to pray for help and guidance, and a man came onto the platform who was in fact an evangelist. He sat with Berry and somehow a shared and very public prayer, with a gathering crowd, led to his being taken in for help by a man who ran a mission hall. In short, Berry found his spiritual redemption on that railway platform; his life was saved and he became a changed man.

He published one more book: a short one called Mr J Berry's *Thoughts Above the Gallows,* published in 1905. It was a tract against hanging and a clear assertion of a path to salvation, willed out of his past life, both public and private. There is a quiet desperation running through everything he wrote, but this final work maintains that thread of eccentricity that was always in him, with a discussion of one of his latest fads, phrenology.

He was then an evangelist, but the paraphernalia of his main occupation lingered on through time, a batch of his possessions being exhibited in a Nottingham junk shop in 1948, and in the 1950s, Berry's granddaughter still had some relics of Berry's to pass on.

James Berry died at Walnut Tree Farm, Bolton, Bradford, on 21 October 1913. It is entirely in keeping with the man and his character that the local obituary should contain an anecdote about Berry trying to sell the cigar-case of a man he had executed. That note of desperation and the need for small profits, while at the same time feeling a sense of the grandeur of his past, sums up one of the puzzles of Berry the hangman – a rare mix of dignity and low life street hawking. He always looked to a quick profit and somehow, as with almost all hangmen in the records, never fully accommodated his professional self with his self-esteem.

He was a man of profound contradictions, with a reputation which attracted the media. As one journalist wrote after hearing Berry talk, 'He subsequently went a-lecturing and in that capacity introduced us to quite a modern pronunciation of the word guillotine. He called it *gelatine* . . .' They liked to laugh at him, though always with a shiver of revulsion.

CHAPTER 10

Bartholomew Binns

In October 1890, at the Middlesex Theatre in London, there was a performance of a piece billed as *The Ghost of Bartholomew Binns*, with a song to match. It would be one of those popular attractions, much like the Punch and Judy shows or the melodramas about the Red Barn murders, or of Charles Peace: transient but at the time very powerful on the general perceptions of the shadowy figure of the hangman. The subject of this chapter was to prove perhaps the most controversial of them all. He began his career with the rope just before the government started taking an interest in the training of executioners and put forward the first guidelines about training. Partly due to Binns's mistakes, those suggested reforms took place after the turn of the century.

We return to the Phoenix Park murders now. This is because Bartholomew Binns was also involved in the following retributions, and he had a very bad press for it. On 6 May 1882 a teenager called James Murphy, of Thomas Street, Dublin, was walking in Phoenix Park in that city. He told a barrister later that he was alone there a little

Bartholomew Binns.
Laura Carter

after seven in the evening and then he saw a strange sight. Here are his own words:

> *I was coming by the sunk trench in front of the Viceregal Lodge . . . I was proceeding towards the gate in the direction of the town . . . I saw a group of persons there who drew my attention. I thought they were wrestling when I perceived them at first . . . When I came up on the road I saw one body lying on the road and the other on the footway. The one on the roadway first fell . . . I think the car man wore a slouched hat . . .*

What the young man's vague description relates to is one of the formative events in Irish history: the murder of Lord Frederick Cavendish, Chief Secretary for Ireland, and his under-secretary, Mr Harry Burke referred to in the previous chapter. The men who had attacked and killed them were brutal in the extreme, as the coroner said, 'The sight of the dead bodies was sufficiently shocking . . . they seem to have been attacked in front, and they seem to have been unarmed and defenceless, within sight of the habituees of the park . . .'

The killings were also to make the most significant experience in the life of Dewsbury executioner, Bartholomew Binns, because subse-

HMP Lincoln today: scene of an early Billington hanging when the nephew stepped in. The author

quently, an informer against the killers, the Irish 'Invincibles' as they were known, had been shot and killed in a ship off South Africa. It became Binns' task to hang the gunman. Marwood had, as we have seen, hanged the first batch, but one killer almost escaped, but being eventually tracked down to that ship, and brought back for trial.

In 1883 the papers were actively promoting discussion and prurient interest into who would succeed Marwood. *The Pall Mall Gazette* for 2 October in that year had this snippet of information:

> *The disappointment of the unsuccessful candidates for the late Mr Marwood's office would (one is afraid) have been heightened had they seen the glowing account which the Figaro had already given of "The Hangman's First Night." The actual succession had passed to Mr Bartholomew Binns, a foreman platelayer in the employ of the Lancashire and Yorkshire Railway Company, and it is satisfactory to learn that he has so far shown a disposition to bear himself modestly and with due reserve. It appears that he arrived at Dewsbury with his full-blown honours fresh upon him on Friday night, but his progress was unofficial and he travelled incognito. A friendly publican was however, in the secret; and this gentleman (perhaps with an eye to business) was not inclined to keep his distinguished visitor too much to himself, and Mr Binns had already held his first reception in the smoke room of the Albion Hotel, Dewsbury. One can only hope that the social duties of his office will be more pressing that the executive . . .*

In that lengthy and arch report, we have the beginning of a sensational relationship with the press that was to dog every stage of Binns' career. There was always a vicarious interest in the profession, of course, and the interesting point is the interest the press had in making sure that the public hangman was 'modest' and showed 'reserve'. Clearly, a public reception in a smoke room was not to be advised.

Binns was carefully monitored as he began as well; the *Reynolds Newspaper* for November 1883 tells of his first job. This was the execution of Henry Powell at Wandsworth prison. The reporter was impressed, writing that, 'All accounts agree in saying that he went about his business in a methodical and hangman-like manner. Most men would have evinced considerable nervousness in performing such a ghastly duty for the first time; but Bartholomew Binns seems to have been perfectly self-possessed and unmoved. We do not bring this against him as a charge. On the contrary, it is comforting to know that the Sheriffs of London have hit upon a person so well qualified to do their unpleasant work for them.' We have to notice here to reference to the fact that Binns was 'hit upon', so implying an element of luck. By the 1880s, training for professionals in general was much discussed, and people were beginning to reflect more deeply on exactly how hangmen had been considered qualified for the post in the past. The usual winning factor was a little experience, as with Calcraft; but Marwood had introduced a truly professional element and that had a knock-on effect in the ideologies of the time.

Yet the press were keen to criticize and undermine Binns. The same reporter noted that Binns had applied for the post 'not for the money it would bring him, but in order to obtain public notoriety'. The general feeling was that Binns had 'attained that position'. The writer commented that 'It might be said that Binns is already a household word. But in exchanging the business of platelaying for that of hangman, he will not benefit to any considerable extent in the pecuniary sense.' The reporter worked out that Binns would average around £130 a year in doing his work, but that was based on £10 per hanging, a figure very low. We have seen that Marwood asked £20. The usual tone of the press writers on Binns was darkly humorous and often scathing, as in these words: 'We hope of course, when he is called upon to strangle anyone, that he will do it skilfully and expeditiously, but at the same time we honestly wish that he will be unable to make a living at his new business. We would prefer to see him die of starvation than to make money hanging his fellow creatures.'

Binns was a Gateshead man who moved to Dewsbury where he kept a shop. He followed Marwood, the man who had revolutionised the trade of hangman in the 1870s, but he was not to be in office very long, being lead hangman rather than assistant for just a year. The reason for that was that he managed to provide a service which was an uneasy mix of smooth professional work and disastrous botched jobs. He must have had qualities that appealed to the selection board, however, as he was one of a large number of applicants. But it was not only in his professional work that he attracted trouble and disagreement. In January 1884 he was on the wrong side of law himself, appearing in court for travelling without a ticket, on a trip between Huddersfield and Dewsbury. As he and his assistant, Alfred Archer, sat in the refreshment room, they were asked to produce a ticket and could not do so. Binns made an excuse, explaining that his notoriety had attracted attention and caused delays. The *Leeds Mercury* reported:

Yesterday, the public executioner, Barthlomew Binns, was summoned before the Mayor and other magistrates at the borough court, Dewsbury, along with Alfred Archer, for defrauding the London and North Western Railway Company . . . when travelling between Huddersfield and Dewsbury without having previously paid the fare. He pleaded not guilty . . . the two defendants were at Huddersfield and returned in the evening . . . on alighting, they did not proceed to the ticket-wicket but went to the refreshment room where they remained twenty minutes. They then left, but were both asked for their tickets . . . The defence was that they were unable to obtain tickets at Huddersfield . . .

But it was with the hanging of Patrick O'Donnell, the killer of the 'grass' from the Phoenix park business, that Binns reached celebrity for a short time. To his credit, his hanging of O'Donnell went well. The report in *The Times* for 18 December 1883, has this account of Binns' participation:

Between a quarter of an hour and ten minutes before the time appointed for the execution, the bell of St Sepulcre's commenced tolling . . . Immediately afterwards the civic officials, accompanied by Captain Sutton Kirkpatrick, the Governor of Clerkenwell and Newgate, and the Rev. Mr Duffield . . . Proceeded to the condemned cell where Bartholomew Binns, the public executioner, who had arrived at Newgate Friday evening, quickly went through the process of pinioning the convict's arms in the ordinary manner . . . . The executioner then secured the pinioning straps around his legs and having adjusted the ropes around the culprit's neck . . . then touching a lever, the body of the unhappy man disappeared from sight.

The reporter was profoundly impressed by Binns' skill, noting that the death had been so instantaneous because, in the surgeon's opinion, there could not even have been 'a twitching of the hands'.

This all counterbalanced the Dutton fiasco in Liverpool, but it certainly made Binns well known. Dutton was responsible for a murder in Athol Street, Liverpool. Just before Christmas 1883, Binns and his assistant arrived in the city and stayed at the *Sessions Hotel*, near Kirkdale gaol. Binns went to the gaol and inspected the scaffold. What was to follow was horrendous, though the *Liverpool Mercury* pointed out that Binns had 'already hanged four men'. The writer said that Binns had been interviewed by the press several times since taking over from Marwood, and Binns told the reporter than he had not seen Dutton at that point; he was described as 'A tall, spare, close-shaven man more than fifty years of age . . . He was dressed in black, wore a billycock hat and appeared to be a decent person of reserved habits and steadiness of nerve.'

What followed was sheer terror. Henry Dutton, an ironworker, had killed Hannah Henshaw, his wife's grandmother, and was due to hang at Kirkdale. There was a special element of drama in the case, as two local journalists were to be present, and also Dutton had asked the

Master Talfourd, an active anti-hanging campaigner at this time. Author's collection

chaplain to give the optional condemned sermon on the Sunday before the fatal hour. The sermon was given, covering three warnings which are totally irrelevant, if not insulting, to a condemned man: not to be drunk, not to allow a bad temper to possess you, and not to marry in haste. Unless these were likely to happen in the next world, the whole affair appears to be cruelly ironic. But in the very early hours of his last day on earth, Dutton had something to eat (cocoa, bread and butter) and took sacrament in the prison chapel.

At seven Binns arrived. For some odd reason, the Governor would not allow Binns' assistant to enter Kirkdale. It was normal practice to have a hangman together with his assistant. But the prison bell began to toll at a quarter to eight and in haste, Dutton was brought to meet Binns and to be pinioned ready for the drop. Then, as the chaplain read some text concerning man's sins, the ritual walk to the scaffold began. The final walk was in line with regulations: the chief warder led the way, followed by Dutton and two warders; then Binns was behind them, followed in line by a doctor, the under-sheriff and the chaplain. So far so good, but then they reached the scaffold.

The drama came when Dutton was given the rapid final pinioning and strapping ready for the lever to be pulled; the clock for eight had not struck, and Binns walked to look at his victim, causing a rather nervous atmosphere. Dutton asked Lord Jesus to receive his soul. Then the clock struck and the lever was pulled; Dutton dropped, but it was not a quick death.

The doctor looked down at the struggling man on the rope and said, 'This is poor work. He is not yet dead.' In a drop of almost seven and a half feet, the body spun around and the man did not die for eight minutes. This was outrageously cruel by any standards. The doctor could see what the problem was: a very thick rope had been used – like a ship's hawser, the doctor said later – and Dutton was very short, only five feet two inches. The result was what every hangman feared: slow strangulation rather than a snapping of the spinal column with speed, and from a humane intention.

There was an inquest after all this farce, with Mr Barker, the county coroner, in charge. The prison governor, Major Leggett, made a long statement outlining the time taken for the culprit to die, and also added that nothing had been done to 'hasten the end' of the unfortunate Dutton. The doctor's evidence would make difficult reading for anyone concerned about the terrible suffering the man experienced; only a slight separation of two bones in the vertebrae near the point of contact with the rope had happened, rather than any sharp break. In the doctor's opinion, the noose had been placed at the wrong position near the nape of the neck, rather than under the jaw or the ear. There was, it was stated, a difference of 300 pounds in the drop to weight ratio. The question must have been on everybody's lips and the coroner asked it – was the executioner sober?

Major Leggett answered that he was not sure. Then an interchange took place that must have ensured Binns's departure from his post:

Coroner: Has the hangman left the gaol?
Leggett: Yes.
Coroner: I wish he were here.

A juryman asked the Governor's opinion of the affair. Leggett said, 'I think it was inefficiently performed – clumsily. I did not like his manner of conducting the execution. He seemed, in adjusting the strap on the man, to do it in a very bungling way, which I did not like at all.'

It was one of the most disgraceful cases of a botched execution in the annals of that grim but necessarily professional task at that period. As Shakespeare said in another context, 'If it were done when 'tis done, then 'twere good it were done well.' The coroner considered the affair to have been a disaster, referring to the fact that 'The

Catherine Flanagan.
Andy Tennick

executioner seemed to be a new hand at the work and that he should have done what the previous man, Calcraft, had done, that is pull on the legs of any man dangling but not swiftly dying.

Oddly, though, Leggett let Binns back into Kirkdale a year later to hang the women poisoners, Catherine Flanagan and Margaret Higgins, who had poisoned several relatives (including children) after taking out life assurance policies on them. This time things went smoothly, as the *Leeds Mercury* reported: 'Five reporters were admitted to the execution. Bartholomew Binns was the executioner, but he was assisted on this occasion by an assistant, a fellow-townsman, Charles Heath . . . The two culprits were more composed than was expected . . . The ropes were quickly adjusted round the necks of the two women, the ropes being placed under the neck in each case and within a few seconds of their arrival on the scaffold the bolt was drawn. Death was apparently instantaneous . . .' It is interesting to note that Leggett was not having any repetition of the Dutton fiasco. The drops for the women were around ten feet, an assistant was allowed, and the placing of the nooses was supervised. Leggett told the press that the execution had been 'regularly and accurately carried out'. Incidentally, Charles Heath (sometimes recorded as Samuel) was from Wakefield and officiated at three hangings.

A week or so later, Binns was assaulted by a plate-layer called William Taylor, working for Binns' former employers. The attack was apparently unprovoked, but may have had something to do with his very low reputation, as well as an altercation over an insult by another man, friendly with Taylor, over money paid in court. The attacker was merely fined a fairly small sum, and one has to note the very liberal treatment of the offender. But the aggressive encounter with Taylor brought out an aspect of Binns' character; he went looking for more trouble at an inn called *The Rising Sun* and threatened two men. Binns had a garden near the railway property and Taylor Green had been accused by Binns of having stolen something from that garden. At the end of the hearing, the Bench dismissed the case, saying they hoped they had heard the last about Binns and his garden.

There is a story that, before the hanging of O'Donnell, a traveller came into Binns' shop and tried to sell song sheets about the imminent death of the 'Invincible' Fenian. When Binns did not buy one, the man went away, only to return in an aggressive mood with threats of shooting Binns. Help was summoned and the man eventually served a prison term.

But the downward spiral in his career, when it came, was speedy. First London removed him from the scene: an announcement in March 1884 stated that 'Alderman Sir Andrew Lusk MP called the attention of the court to the subject of the appointment of Bartholomew Binns to the office of hangman, and in view of what had recently taken place with reference to him, moved that the 20 guineas honorarium paid to him annually should be withdrawn.' It was withdrawn; what had happened just before that sacking was that, after

Margaret Higgins.
Andy Tennick

another bungled hanging in Liverpool (of McLean) he was relieved of duties in the north. He had arrived at Walton drunk and had had to be helped by a man called Samuel Heath, to complete the job.

The petty troubles and squabbles that filled Binns' life continued to the end; he had a nasty side to him, as he not only took his mother-in-law to court over alleged theft, but also, so the story went at the time, he tended to hang cats and dogs for some kind of horrible pleasure. Apparently his mother-in-law reported him for that. His final years were pathetically miserable and he even tried to earn a few pounds at fairs and feasts, explaining execution methods. In fact, in 1889, he was in court again, this time at Sheffield County Court, claiming arrears of wages from the showman, Thomas Whitely, totalling £9.2s. Binns was described dismissively in the press as a man who had 'occasionally acted as hangman'. One report said that he had been travelling around with Whitely, 'exhibiting himself as public executioner' showing the public how hangings were done. He failed to get the money but was allowed to sue again. Binns did so, as that was his nature.

The media were not finished with him, though. The *Pall Mall Gazette*, which had taken against him from the start, noted that matters of hanging in Austria were done with more dash and colour: 'In the first place, the hangman should be invested with some of the majesty of the law; and just as a judge of the assize has his ermine and his trumpeters, so the minister of the law's last decree should be attired in a showy uniform, with a cocked hat and jack boots. Mr Bartholomew Binns would, we do not doubt, have no objection to this part of the Austrian system . . .'

It has to be asserted that the *Gazette* was probably right; for all their tormenting and teasing him in their columns, they had realised early on that Binns loved the rather suspect popularity of his office and they did not want to let him forget how morally questionable that stance was.

CHAPTER 11

Throttler Smith

George Smith's photograph shows a man with a resolute expression and a firm mouth. He seems like a man who had stoicism and fortitude. He may not have attracted the notoriety of Calcraft and Binns, but he was busy as a hangman, notably in the West Midlands, and if for nothing else, he will go down in crime history as the man who hanged the Rugeley poisoner, William Palmer. Smith was born in 1805 at Rowley Regis near Birmingham, and although he was from a good, solidly Victorian family, he was something of a ruffian in his early years, and worked in gangs doing petty crime.

He married young and that does not seem to have forced him into regular work; he was imprisoned several times at Stafford for theft, and never really found what he wanted to do in life until the fancy of being hangman attracted him, and he managed to become assistant to William Calcraft, who used various assistants at times, including Evan Evans of Carmarthen, a man who changed his name to Robert Anderson because he was known as 'Evans the Hangman'. The first work he did alone was of James Owen and George Thomas outside Stafford gaol in 1840.

Throttler Smith.
Chris Wade

As private executions came in after 1868, Smith worked at times with Calcraft to learn the trade with rather less pressure than was normal at a public event. The first of these was the hanging of young Thomas Wells at Maidstone. Wells was a teenage railway porter who had killed his superior at Priory Station, Dover, after being told he was insolent and slack in his work. Wells loaded an old gun and shot Mr Walsh. There was no defence: it was murder. Wells was on the scaffold at Maidstone on 13 August 1868 and George Smith prepared him, using a hempen ring on his neck.

After that, Calcraft and Smith worked at Durham, hanging Alexander Mackay. Smith, who wore a velveteen jacket, suggesting he was something of a dandy, and it was none too successful, as a reporter commented that 'signs of life were visible for a longer time after the bolt was drawn than we remember to have seen previously . . .' Then in August 1872, Calcraft and Smith presided at a triple execution at Newgate. Smith was by that time a well-seasoned professional.

The sure sign that Smith was a real professional was in evidence at the hanging of wife-killer Samuel Twigg in 1861. Twigg lived in Bilston, marrying Mary Walton in 1845 and settling down to life as a bricklayer. But Twigg was a heavy drinker as well as a hard worker; he tended to become violent when in his cups, and by 1860, after his fighting had landed him in gaol a few times, he was heard to say about his wife, 'One day I'll finish her for good.' On 24 July 1860, he went on a binge and came home roaring drunk, hammering on the door. When he and a drunken friend demanded food, Mary didn't co-operate and Twigg became threatening to her. Luckily for the wife, Twigg soon slept, falling asleep on the floor, but as Mary took a light downstairs for their son, Twigg asked for a kiss and then stabbed his wife in the stomach.

People tried to help, but she was clearly bleeding to death. First the doctor and then the constable arrived, and Twigg was arrested. The locals outside shouted 'Hang the bastard!' That is exactly what happened. There was an appeal for a reprieve but at eight in the morning of 5 January 1861, he walked onto the scaffold in front of a huge crowd of several thousand, many of them being there after taking special trains. Smith was quick with the pinion and hood, and there was a massive swell of shouting and booing as the lever was pulled and Twigg slid down to his death. He was, as the custom dictated for such felons, quicklimed in the coffin and buried in the prison grounds. Smith was a true professional.

Throttler Smith, as he became known did jobs at Norwich as well as at Stafford. He was to make mistakes, as all the other hangmen did, but when it came to the really high-profile victim of his skills, William

Palmer, he did the task well. Palmer poisoned fourteen people, all in order to gather some cash to feed his gambling habit. The gambling was unsuccessful and the debts mounted; although he was a fairly successful physician in Rugeley, setting up his practice in 1846, he had a wild streak which included fathering several bastards and following slow horses at the courses. Murder was the simplest way out of his problems, he thought, and so he began to use his knowledge of drugs and poisons to see off all kinds of people.

His first victim was his mother-in-law, who had come to live with his family in 1848; she died soon after arriving and her possessions and cash went to Mrs Palmer – which meant effectively that Palmer had the money to spend of course. By 1854 deaths in the Palmer household were more frequent than the average, even in that time when infant mortality was high. By that year, four children and an uncle had died in the house; when his wife died, he was left a very large sum of money, and the income from insurance firms was considerable. But the gambling went on, and after the doctor's brother died the insurance people became suspicious and refused to pay out yet again.

What eventually caught him out was the death of his gambling friend, John Cook. They had both had a day out at Shrewsbury races and when they came home they went for drinks, as Cook had made some money (Palmer had lost as usual). But when Cook was ill at the party, and was subsequently treated by Palmer before he died, the suspicions around the doctor's circle were too positive and rabid to ignore. The law paid him a visit and he was charged with murder. He had to be tried in London, such was the local hatred. In May 1856 he stood in the dock at the Old Bailey. It was a most notorious case. The *Daily Telegraph* reported on 27 May:

> *Each day since Palmer was first arraigned at the bar of the Old Bailey, among all classes of society, from the ennobled peer down to the most humble of London costermongers, there has been one grand prevailing desire to hear the trial, and if possible, to obtain a glimpse of the Rugeley hero of poisoning notoriety. Every morning has attracted crowds of spectators to the vicinity . . . from Ludgate Hill to Newgate prison there was a dense crowd of people prior to the opening of the court . . .*

When he was sentenced and the prospect of such a celebrity villain being hanged was appreciated, the fervour was uncontainable in the media. The public had also learned a good deal about the nature of strychnine, Palmer's chosen poison. Letters to *The Times* and other papers educated the readers on this, on several occasions. One writer noted that 'In proof of the correctness of the pinion that strychnine remains in the bodies of animals killed by it, permit me to quote a single instance . . . . On a fox being found dead and the proprietor of the covert being blamed for it, on enquiry it appeared that some hens' eggs had been contaminated with strychnine, that a rook and magpie and eaten these . . . and then been eaten by the fox . . .'

On Saturday 14 June at eight in the morning, Throttler Smith executed Palmer at Stafford. Barriers had been placed in the main road and in the street where the scaffold was placed. As well as 150 of the regular police force of the county, a large number of special constables was assembled. The authorities were well aware that a huge crowd would gather. The *Daily Telegraph* set the scene:

The inns of Stafford drove a busy trade on Friday. All day long, people flocked into the town, by road, by rail, on foot, on horseback, in gig, carriage or on donkey. Such crowding at the railway station, such jostling in the tavern yards, tavern parlours and coffee rooms, such crowding and pushing in public houses . . . Beds had been at a premium for days before, for everybody wanted to get shelter . . . There was no bed to be got, not for love nor money . . .

People with an eye to business had provided stands which would be good viewing points for the hanging; costs for these ranged from five shillings to a guinea. Primitive Methodists arrived to walk with banners proclaiming 'Prepare to Meet Thy God' and walked around with papers warning of the dangers of gambling.

The press took a deep interest in the condemned man's last week in the gaol, noting all visitors; Palmer's brothers and sister went to see him, and he would not see his one remaining son. The press commented: 'The poor child, it appears, is still at Rugeley with his grandmother; he has been informed that his father has gone to some distant part of the country and is anxious for his return . . .' The chaplain was with Palmer most of the night, and readers were told that Palmer had a cup of tea but nothing to eat, and said that he was prepared for the ordeal.

Throttler Smith was naturally a figure of intense interest to the reporters. Some writers got his name wrong, referring to him as John; it was stated that 'he was dressed in a very clean white smock-frock; he is a remarkably thick-set, robust looking man, apparently between fifty and sixty years old . . . he carries on some little labouring trade in the town of Dudley.' Some facts given were wrong, such as one report that he had only done a few other hangings. As usual, enquiries about the hangman's fee were made and it was aid that he had a flat fee of five pounds plus expenses.

The accounts of the hanging present a remarkably controlled and smooth job, despite the fact that 25,000 people were watching from various places and distances. The *Telegraph* wrote:

> *The hangman, having drawn the cap over the face of the prisoner, retired from the scaffold and withdrew the bolt that secured the drop, which fell, and he appeared to die instantly. There was not a single convulsive effort observable, his pinioned hands gradually dropped, and he ceased to exist apparently without a pang. His hands, which had presented a white, plump appearance, had turned blue, indeed almost black . . . The awful silence which prevailed was terrible . . .*

Such a high-profile celebrity killer was the subject of more interest even after death. After hanging for an hour, the body was cut down and then a cast of Palmer's head was taken by a man from the Liverpool Phrenological Society.

Palmer was buried within the area of the gaol. Ironically, people had gambled on whether or not Palmer would hang; betting types took odds of 12 to 1 that he would not hang. In keeping with the killer's poor gambling, it was made known that he had placed a massive bet on a horse called Yellow Jack in the Derby that year. He would have lost his £400.

As for Smith, near the end of his working life he was to experience a fiasco similar to the Liverpool Dutton story. This was the case of Christopher Edwards. This was yet another wife killing. Edwards was a locksmith from Willenhall, aged thirty-four. He had knifed his wife. The hanging turned out to be a highly irregular affair. At first it seemed that things had progressed quite normally, as the lever was pulled and Edwards' body hung on the rope. But just as the officials were ready to accept it was a clean job, the body began moving; Edwards moved like a fish in shallow water, jerking about and struggling for life. It was four minutes before he died.

Smith had had another bad experience in 1866 with a man called Collier. This was at Stafford, and Collier was a poacher who had killed a local worthy; the rope slipped away from the overhead beam at the first attempt, and Smith had to take the man down so that the chaplain could talk to him, while another rope was rigged. As a second attempt was begun, the crowd was restless and abusive: there was around five minutes lapse of time between the two hangings, and it is not clear how much the poor culprit knew about all this.

This was the end of the line for Throttler. After all, he was sixty-seven. As with so many other hangmen, he was something of a local celebrity of course. He spent his last years thirty miles from Stafford, at Tividale, and he died in 1874. He was sixty-nine and it seems that, again with a feature of the hangman's declining years, drink played a part in his death. His son, another George, did a few hangings as assistant, but did not progress. There was no chance of there being a dynasty as was the case with the Billingtons and the Pierrepoints. But the Victorian world knew the name of Throttler Smith, forever linked with the Rugeley poisoner. In fact, he had proved to be one of the mentally toughest on record, enjoying a general good regard with the public. Comparisons with the abuse suffered by Binns make that clear. He did have one difficult experience, though, as he was waiting for a train to Birmingham after hanging a man called Price. The *Warwick and Warwickshire Advertiser* tells the tale: 'He had a bundle of clothes in his hand which were supposed to be those which Price wished to be given to the mother of the murdered girl, but which proved to be a suit of his own. He stood on the edge of the platform and a strong fellow mounted the balustrade, jumped on him, and bore him down onto the line, to which some twenty or thirty other men soon made their way . . . The 12.50 goods train, which does not stop at Warwick, had not arrived . . . Some of the ring-leaders threatened to push the executioner under the engine when it came up.' They were after revenge on him because he had not let Price finish his prayers before pulling the lever. Smith was saved by the intervention of the station master.

CHAPTER 12

Billington Tales

Following the enquiries and debate about hangmen and training in the 1880s, a memorandum was issued in 1891 on 'instructions for carrying out an execution'. This document was the result of both the bunglings of Binns and the long-standing critical lobby in parliament against the barbarity of the death penalty. Another influence on this was the nature of executions throughout the Empire. By the closing years of the century, the regional hangings done by district magistrates in such places as India, were being questioned too, as the nature of military rule changed.

The memo gave detailed instructions about duties over a timescale that covered a preparation period as well as the scaffold work itself. For instance, this was the note on procedure which came as part of the worry about ropes: 'After the completion of each test the scaffold and all the appliances will be locked up, and the key kept by the Governor . . . but the bag of sand should be suspended all the night preceding the execution so as to take the stretch out of the rope.' In other words, the science and the craft of hanging was encoded. The only thing that could not be described and passed on was the professional behaviour in the 'turning off' work. That was still open to both use and abuse.

Billington is a name that was all over the papers for several years, such was the dominance of the Billington hangmen from Lancashire. The dynasty began with sheer amateur cheek and progressed through to extreme professionalism, with plenty of incidents along the way.

A social documentarist venturing into Newgate for some interesting 'copy' met James Billington and gave a picture of the execution shed. He noted that 'from the condemned cell to the place of execution is not more than 40 feet' and that Billington was the man impressively in control: 'I never hope to experience this awful, ignominious and brutal death . . . Who knows, the writer may be a great man some day if he escapes Mr Billington . . . The hanging performed by Mr Billington leaves nothing to be desired.' He sarcastically goes on to say that the dead felons, could they do so, would provide a 'certificate of merit' to the hangman. It would seem, then, that in James Billington, the first of a long dynasty of hangmen from that family in Lancashire, was most successful and that his name is not attached to any farces or bunglings.

James Billington.
Laura Carter

Though a Bolton man, as Steve Fielding has written, he replaced Berry and that 'it was unusual for the normally thrifty Yorkshiremen to employ a Lancashire man, who would have to travel and therefore run up an expenses account . . .' But it did happen, and for eight years he was the man who became quite a familiar sight at Armley gaol, busy in the execution shed there. He had been married twice, having been born in Bolton in 1847. His first wife, Alice Pennington, died in 1890, aged only forty; they lost three children, including a little girl called Polly. One of the few anecdotes we have of him that show us the ordinary, human side of the man is the tale that, after his daughter's death, her schoolfriends brought a wreath for her and the future hangman was overcome with grief, saying, 'See, I'd sooner have lost £5 than ha' lost her!'

He first worked in the mills as a piecer and then he sang in clubs and pubs before entering the retail trade (as many hangmen did) as a barber at Farnworth. James was, even when very young, interested in the macabre subject of execution, and he used to experiment with a dummy, done to death from a home-made scaffold constructed in the backyard where they lived at Higher Market Street in Farnworth.

As he was rooted in that community, cutting hair and no doubt chatting about holidays and work as barbers tend to do, he had to try to avoid the morbid curiosity aroused by his other job. His shop obviously attracted journalists and he tried to travel under a guise of anonymity too. He was known as Higgins when out on execution business, very smart and presentable. This would be the man met and respected by the reporter in Newgate, who had no doubt gone there partly in search of this quiet professional 'in his lair'.

He had long wanted to be a hangman, and had applied at the same time as Berry, wanting Marwood's position. He was to be in office for seventeen years, from 1884 to 1901. After the application, Billington was called to York where he was interviewed and asked to describe what method he would use to hang people. When he first began he worked near London, employed to work in the London and Home Counties. But he started work at Armley in 1884, hanging Joseph Laycock. Laycock was a worker at Kelham Island in Sheffield and was always a problem to someone. From being very young he lived by his fists and by indulging in petty crime. When he married Maria Green she probably had no idea what a problem she had saddled herself with, and they soon had a large family, four children born by 1884. Maria's life was desperately deprived and tough. Laycock was often away as he was a militiaman (and also sometimes behind bars) and the young wife even had to resort to collecting bottles to make ends meet.

The couple were settled in White Croft and their relationship was more than stormy – in fact it was deathly perilous. Laycock had a homicidal streak and the local community knew that. Maria's way of coping was to drink heavily, so matters degenerated rapidly. He assaulted her and did a spell in gaol for it. But not long after that, two men saw Laycock early in the morning, looking agitated. Mysteriously, there was no sound from the Laycock home for some time after that. Neighbours and Maria's mother eventually realised that something dreadful had happened, and they saw Maria lying dead, her head almost off her shoulders. They called for the police.

In the Laycock house the officers found the man with his throat cut, not dead, but wanting to expire. He had cut the throats of all four of his children. When he was well enough to stand trial, the common problem in these cases was to emerge: was he insane? Lawyers throughout the nineteenth century increasingly found themselves having to try to construct a defence of insanity in these instances, and it was always difficult to do so. In the case of Laycock, it was known that his father and his uncle had both taken their own lives. The judge was of the opinion that this was not the act of a sane man, but the jury disagreed.

Laycock's response to the death sentence was: 'Thank you, your worship, thank you.' After inspection by medical men, out to verify the point about genetic insanity, resulted in their insisting that there was no such influence in this case. He was to be a victim of Billington.

It was a blessed release, one might argue. When it came near to the time he was to be taken to be hanged, his resolve weakened and he was weeping, overcome by the desperate situation, when Billington came to the cell. Laycock asked, pleadingly, 'Thou'lt not hurt me?' The report of the conversation was written in such a way that Billington's Bolton accent was attempted: 'Theaull be eawt of existence in two minutes.' But Laycock collapsed and had to be helped to the noose. As Billington fixed the rope where he wanted it, the condemned man spoke his last words: 'Oh my children, my children. Lord have mercy on my children.'

Billington's record of executions went far beyond Yorkshire, though. He was the man who hanged Amelia Dyer at Newgate, who had murdered a four-month-old child. She had been one of the people involved in the so-called 'baby farming' scandal at the time, probably killing at least six babies, purely for the money. But his most famous (or infamous) client was arguably the poisoner, Dr Neil Cream, at Newgate, in 1892.

Cream was born in Scotland but he emigrated to Canada in the 1850s. After graduating in medicine he started practice in Chicago, but he was fond of using poison and had a streak of homicidal tendency in him, poisoning his mistress's husband in 1881 and when released ten years later from Joliet prison he went to London and indulged his psychopathic desires by attracting prostitutes whom he could use for experiments with strychnine.

But the bad doctor liked notoriety and enjoyed the risk of being found – a common trait in serial killers. He even went to the police to tell them that not only was he in danger of attack but that he knew the identity of the killer who had been dubbed 'The Lambeth Poisoner' (himself of course). Not long after, following a spell back in America, he returned to London and while doing his nefarious experiments, he was described by a survivor and of course, arrested. A woman pretended to have taken pills, knowing the danger she was in, and went to fetch the law. The officers found seven bottles of strychnine at his home. The next step was to court, and after that, Newgate to await execution.

James Billington, along with others present at the scaffold, heard the doctor say, 'I am Jack the . . .' just as he was 'dropped'. But of course, he was in Joliet gaol at the time of the Whitechapel murders.

Most of Billington's hangings were full of incident, but few so chaotic as the triple hangings at Newgate in 1899 when an assistant called Warbrick and a whole crowd of warders were present at the scaffold following a brawl in the courtroom at their trial. Billington did not have a proper view of everyone involved and he pulled the lever while Warbrick was still pinioning one of the felons. The assistant fell down the trap with the three killers, and he had the wit to grab one of the pairs of legs to break his fall.

As with all the hangmen, James had to keep plying another trade, and he took a public house called the *Derby Arms* in Bolton. He married again in 1891, a woman called Alice Fletcher, the daughter of a local greengrocer. But before we leave the account of the first Billington, there is one more job he did that has to be told. This relates to the man in Oscar Wilde's great poem, *The Ballad of Reading Gaol*, who killed the one he loved:

> *He did not pass in purple pomp*
> *Nor ride a moon-white steed,*
> *Three yards of cord and a sliding board*
> *Are all the gallows need.*
> *So with rope of shame the herald came*
> *To do the secret deed.*

The murderer in question whom Wilde saw and knew was trooper Thomas Wooldridge, who had killed his wife, Laura Ellen, by cutting her throat, at Clewer, near Windsor. James Billington hanged Wooldridge on 7 July 1896. The soldier was in the Royal Horse Guards, and Wilde dedicated his poem to him:

> *In Memoriam C.T.W.*
> *Sometime trooper of the Royal Horse Guards*
> *Obit H.M. Prison,*
> *Reading, Berkshire*
> *7th July, 1896*

James' period on the Home Office list ended in 1901; there were several other Billingtons who were hangmen in a long dynasty, but none of them were specifically hangmen appointed for Yorkshire as James was. But what happened was that the family – Thomas, who died young but was assistant, John and William – did some executions in Yorkshire. Most notable was William, the second of James' three sons. He performed a number of executions in his short period in office (1902–5) and in the records of these, one in particular gives us a vivid picture of the Billingtons at work: this was a hanging in Ruthin in February 1903.

William Hughes had been in the Cheshire Regiment and had served in the Empire; he returned in 1890 and worked as a collier near Wrexham. He married Jane Williams in 1892, but after a few years (and the death of one of his sons) matter between them degenerated and he left her. Jane had to work as a housekeeper and William was

convicted for desertion of his family. There was a burning jealousy in
William as he knew that his wife was now with a man called
Maddocks. Intending to kill both his wife and her lover, he arrived at
the Maddocks house with a shotgun. When he learned that Maddocks
was not there, he shot both barrels into his wife and then shortly after
gave himself up to the police.

Ruthin gaol is a small, oppressive place (now a crime museum) and
it had a small execution shed behind. The authorities had worked out
the logistics of hanging, as a contemporary account explains: 'The
prisoner occupies as his death cell, two cells which had been knocked
into one . . . The cell was about fifteen yards or so from the scaffold
so that he had only a short distance to walk. In the wall of the prison
a hole had been knocked through, which led onto the second storey of
the gallows . . .'

Into this small, quiet market town came the Billington brothers,
William and John. The *Denbighshire Free Press* had this account of
them:

> *Great curiosity was evinced both in Denbigh and in Ruthin to see the
> hangman Billington . . . From appearances no one would think for a
> moment the two quiet-looking, pale-faced persons attired in dark suits,
> with bowler hats, were the men who would be chief actors in the
> launching of a human being into eternity . . . They bore absolutely no
> luggage . . . that had been forwarded to the prison to await them . . .
> Upon arrival at the jail Billington had hardly put his hand upon the bell
> when the attentive warder opened the door and admitted them . . .*

It must have been a difficult night, even for the two professionals,
as they slept 'very close to the condemned cell where their prisoner
was sleeping his last earthly sleep . . .' It is a small local gaol, with
narrow corridors and low roofed cells and offices. It would not be
going too far to imagine that they heard Hughes snore – if he slept at
all that night.

But the main point here is the bland, restrained efficiency and
bearing the hangmen had. The Billingtons took their trade seriously
and planned everything well. The local reporter appears to have
known everything they did, pointing out that Billington 'announced
everything to be in perfect order before he retired early'. As for the
prisoner, he simply asked for one last thing – to see a photograph of
his family looking happy, and that was granted.

William's most celebrated victim was Samuel Dougal, of the Moat
House Farm case in Chelmsford. Dougal had killed and buried Camille
Holland at the farm and it had taken detectives a long time to find her
body in a trench. The importance of that case with regard to hanging

was that there was an incident on the scaffold involving the chaplain. The Reverend Blakemore had a strong desire to ascertain the truth for moral and religious reasons, in his capacity of attendant chaplain. But he stepped over the line of protocol and good sense when he delayed the whole proceedings for some time, asking Dougal, who was standing on the trapdoor with the hood over his head, if he was guilty or not guilty. There was a delay, but the man was heard to say the word 'guilty' a split-second before the lever was pulled. This led to a scandal, and finally to a reform in legally-sanctioned procedure, barring chaplain's from interfering with the work of professionals in the penal service. Billington must have been patient that day.

William also hanged a sailor from Durham called John Sullivan. It was a case in which the defence of unsound mind was tried, because in the navy he had suffered heart problems and also depression. It did him no good at all. What Sullivan did was murder a friend and shipmate called Lowthian with an axe. It was well documented that Sullivan had an intimate relationship with the other man, and his closeness had transmuted into a crazy obsessive desire to control. He had been seen holding a knife to the man's throat, and then later he held an axe and talked about murder. One night, as Lowthian was chatting to a friend, the killer approached and sliced him with the axe. There was some kind of basis for a defence case, because rambling, mad letters were found in the killer's belongings, and he was totally deranged for some time before the attack.

The author of the Billington story – Mrs Van der Elst, stopping the events on hanging day. Author's collection

But at the trial in June 1904, his defence counsel, Arthur Hutton, lost the case and Judge Grantham gave the death sentence. William and John officiated at Pentonville on 12 July.

There is considerable confusion about the sources of information for William Billington. A book printed in the 1940s has this in a chapter on executioners:

THE MADNESS OF BILLINGTON

William Billington was public executioner. In 1925 he went mad and murdered his wife and two of their children, then killing himself.

This was written by Violet Van Der Elst, a militant campaigner for the abolition of hanging. It seems that someone was in a muddle here, as that fact seems to apply to the Rochdale hangman, John Ellis.

Regardless of all this, the fact is that William was a busy man in the years between 1902–05. The last hanging at Newgate was of George Woolfe and William saw to that. Woolfe was convicted of killing his girlfriend, and he proved to be the last of 1,169 felons hanged at the famous old London gaol, since the gallows were placed there instead of Tyburn in 1783. Only three months after that death, Newgate was demolished. It had long been thought that the old place was not suitable for modern prison work, especially that of execution.

The main chroniclers of hangmen in Britain agree that William lived from 1873 to 1934. Yet the Billington family historian has him born in 1875 in Standish. What that historian does explain is that there were indeed family problems around William and his wife but not murder or suicide. In July 1905 he was charged with failing to maintain his wife and two children; they were taken into the Bolton workhouse as a result. He was given a month's hard labour in gaol. There was further trouble and he had a second sentence later. The real muddle comes with the note in the family history on the web site that 'William died on 2 March 1952 in his early 60s.' If he was born in 1875, that is clearly wrong.

William's life is a mystery in some ways, but what is clear in terms of the work of the Billingtons, execution was often difficult and sometimes sensational. The most important factor in this here is the event of 1899 in Lincoln. There, when James was booked to do a job, he was too ill and William went in his place. Amazingly, the astonished Governor allowed matters to proceed. William told the Governor that he had experience when in fact he had not, and was not on the official list until three years later. He had to tell the Prison Commission that he had performed an execution while not sanctioned by the Home Office.

Another Billington scandal was one involving a mysterious character called 'Warbrick' who ran a campaign of hatred against William, at one point writing to the Home Secretary, sending a newspaper cutting with an account of William being convicted for assault. But Warbrick did act as a very capable assistant most of the time.

CHAPTER 13

The Man from Rochdale

John Ellis was in office between 1901 and 1923, and in that period was responsible for the deaths of several of the most infamous criminals in the chronicles of British crime. Among his notorious clients are Herbert Armstrong, Dr Crippen, George Smith and Sir Roger Casement. He also had to hang women, notably Edith Thompson and Susan Newell. The latter was the first woman to hang in Scotland for more than half a century. Ellis eventually took his own life, and we have his autobiography, a work that includes his reflections on hanging women and also on the very famous clients he had during his career, a time in which he hanged 203 people.

John Ellis. Laura Carter

As well as his own book, *Diary of a Hangman*, we have Jack Doughty's detailed life of Ellis, *The Rochdale Hangman*, published in 1998. For present purposes, I will concentrate on the most notorious of his cases, and bring out the controversy surrounding them. His own memoirs were dictated, and then formed into a book with the help of other writers, mainly T J Leech. In those reflections, Ellis, a gaunt, solemn man with a bushy moustache, gives the reader a special insight into the process of becoming the public hangman in the Edwardian period. He started as assistant to William Billington, and he said that he applied after talking with his workmates about hanging one day and he said, 'That's the kind of job I'd like.' He did not tell his wife that he had applied, so he had to explain the letter from the Home Office that dropped through the letterbox, inviting him to go to Newgate to learn the craft. His reasons for the application are not clear; he wrote:

> *Whatever the reason for it, it certainly wasn't for any love of the grue-some. I've never been that sort of chap. I couldn't kill a chicken, and once when I tried to drown a kitten I was so upset for the rest of the day that my mother said that I was never to be given a similar job again.*

But off he went to London, and there Chief Warder Scott showed him the hangman's room in the prison; he practised on a dummy person and learned about calculating drops and how to pinion someone. He reflected that the Newgate scaffold was taken to Pentonville after the prison was demolished in 1898. 'I used it to execute Dr Crippen, Seddon, Casement and many others, he said, 'It still remained one of the finest scaffolds in the country, and four men could be executed at one time on it . . .'

His career started when he was an assistant at the hanging of John Robert Miller who had killed a man in a fight. From William Billington he learned the right way on that occasion. It was a smooth job. William made it plain that studying the felons was the important part: 'We went to look at the two men, for the condition of their necks and their general physique . . . Young Miller had been behaving in a truculent way . . .' But on the day of the hanging, the deaths were swift, and the two hangmen took a brandy with the Governor after. It was the first hanging that he had seen, too.

Hanging Edith Thompson was something that deeply affected Ellis; he had hanged a woman before, Edith Swann, in Leeds. He wrote about them both in his memoirs. The Thompson case was the classic murdered husband in a love triangle template. The Thompsons lived a regular, hard-working life, and then she fell in love with Frederick Bywaters, a handsome young man who worked as a laundry steward with the P & O line. In October 1922, as the Thompsons were walking

home from a West End show, Bywaters came out of the dark and
stabbed Mr Thompson to death. Both Edith and Freddy were
condemned to hang, and then the nation realised what a terrible
thought that was – to hang a woman. Ellis was the man caught in the
middle of that furore. He had a job to do.

Ellis recalled the hanging very clearly, and he wrote about Edith and
Emily Swann and Sarah Newell. He said of the two working class
women: 'Both these women were coarse and rather vulgar, very
different from Edith Thompson. Although that distinction shouldn't
tell in her favour, it undoubtedly did so with the millions of Britons,
who without concerning themselves unduly with the executions of the

Hilldrop Crescent. Author's collection

first two women, held up their hands in horror when Mrs Thompson was sent to the scaffold.'

Ellis flew from Manchester airport to London for that job, and then was taken to Holloway where there was a massive crowd outside. He had to give a lot of thought to the intricacies of hanging a woman. He had extra help although he had never asked for it; his main recommendation was that the woman be given a large brandy, and he had a chair handy in case she had to be carried out and passed out before the rope was placed. When he first saw her she was 'a pitiable sight' and when she saw him, she behaved with dignity. Ellis realised to his horror that her cell was very near the execution shed, and that she would hear all the noisy preparations. But nothing could be done to change that. He calculated a drop of six feet ten inches, and then tried to relax and sleep.

In the end, it was extremely efficient; as Ellis said, 'One flick of my wrist and Mrs Thompson disappeared from view. She died instantaneously and painlessly . . .' Bywaters was hanged the same day at Pentonville. And he had written a statement declaring her innocent. Ellis was undoubtedly very distressed at what he had had to do. But there was another shock due to him when he got home, because he read that the aircraft he had flown to London in had crashed and three people had died.

The controversy about the Thompson and Bywaters case rages on, and the business has been the subject of fact and fiction in all kinds of contexts. The source of much of that is explained by Robin Odell, who has written: 'Many of the letters which Edith had written to Bywaters were used in evidence at their trial at the Old Bailey in December 1922. Her suggestion that he might become jealous and do something desperate was offered as incitement to murder. The judge, Mr Justice Shearman, delivered a hostile summing-up, dismissing any romantic notions about Edith's relationship with Bywaters. He said they were trying a 'vulgar and common crime'.

The hanging of Dr Crippen is also wreathed in doubt and drama now, after new developments regarding his wife, whom he allegedly murdered in their home and buried under the floor in the cellar. Ellis said, 'The only time I ever regretted being a hangman was during the Crippen case.'

The basic facts are that Crippen was hanged for the murder of his wife, singer Belle Elmore, at 39 Hilldrop Crescent, in London. He was having an affair with his secretary, Ethel Le Neve, and he had spread a tale around their circle of friends that Belle had gone home to America for a funeral. Crippen and Ethel (with her in disguise) boarded the SS *Montrose* when the hunt was on for them, trying to travel to the USA, but they were recognised by the captain, and he sent a wireless message – the first time this was done to clinch a murder hunt – and they were arrested. There was convincing forensic evidence, given by Sir Bernard Spilsbury, at the trial at the Old Bailey, and Crippen was sentenced to death. Ethel went to gaol but was later acquitted.

Inspector Dew, who made mistakes in the Crippen case. Laura Carter

Ellis reported that Crippen died with a smile. He wrote, talking about that massive case with huge media attention, 'It got so bad that I dare hardly venture out of my own house . . . I was just too popular. After all, he was the man who was going to hang 'that monster'. But on the day before his death, Crippen planned to take his own life, smashing his glasses to that he could cut his throat with a shard of glass. His attempt was discovered, as a vigilant warder saw that the glasses were not where they usually were. A search of the bed found them.

But Crippen was up early, ready to die. Ellis wrote that the man had a 'set, calm expression' and that the warders were more upset than he. The world waited for a confession from him; he had protested his innocence throughout. No confession was ever proved to have been made. When he walked to the scaffold, he was smiling. Ellis recalled:

As I stood on the scaffold I could see the procession coming into view . . . Behind the praying priest came the notorious Dr Crippen. If he had ever shown cowardice or collapse, he displayed none now.

Such was Crippen's profile across the newspapers of the world that Ellis was offered the then massive sum of £1,000 to do a lecture tour of America, talking about hanging

The first Ripper murder – Dew was involved in that investigation. Famous Crimes, 1900

Crippen. Ellis refused. He had had a demanding November in 1910 – hanging four poisoners.

The story of Sir Roger Casement is another tale that has spawned libraries of books and articles. He was an Irish nationalist from Dublin, who went into the British Foreign Service in 1892, and was knighted for his humanitarian work in 1911. He joined the Gaelic league and became an Irish Volunteer in 1913. Not only did he try to raise an Irish brigade in Germany, went to Ireland on a German submarine in 1916, and was then arrested. He was charged with high treason.

The great lawyer F E Smith led the prosecution against him, and Casement was sentenced to death. He had been charged with the kind of treason known as 'adhering to the King's enemies' – a law going back to the thirteenth century. As Smith wrote later: ' . . . it was contended that this was an offence that could only be committed by a person present in this country. If this were true . . . than Casement had committed no offence. The defence were confronted by the fact that not only was there an unbroken line of legal opinion, from the sixteenth century onwards, dead in their teeth, but such decisions as there were, were necessarily few because such offenders took care to remain out of reach, were also against them.' In other words, casement was in a ship, close to the land within the King's domain, and was still obviously 'physically present' on British soil.

It was hard for the public at the time to gather any sympathy for Casement: this was made worse by the publication of extracts from his diaries, which showed him to be homosexual, something of course, vilified at the time, and only in Ireland was he a hero. His request for his body to be sent back to Ireland was refused, but in 1965 the body was exhumed and taken to Glasnevin cemetery in Dublin.

Casement died bravely. When Ellis and his assistant went to him in the cell to pinion him, he stood, unmoved, a tall and dignified man, offering no resistance or any trouble. Casement prayed, with Father McCarroll, all the way to the noose; his last words were, 'God save Ireland' and 'Jesus receive my soul.' The official posting of evidence of sentence and death was on the prison door, saying:

I, P R Mander, surgeon of His Majesty's Prison of Pentonville, hereby certify that I this day examined the body of Roger David Casement, on whom judgement of death was this day executed at this prison, and on this examination I found that the said Roger Casement was dead. Dated this third day of August 1916.

Feckless and stupid people may have died on scaffolds in British history, but there were real monsters among the hanged, and one of these was certainly George Joseph Smith, the 'Brides in the Bath' murderer. Smith was born in Bethnal Green in 1872, and was a criminal from his youth, being in the reform school for stealing when he was only nine. Later, as a teenager, he did six months' hard labour for stealing a bicycle. He was then in the army until 1896, and then he began a double life, with the use of aliases and a horrible need to ingratiate and rob all the women he could – choosing easy prey of course. But matters escalated when his violence came through.

When he met Beatrice Munday he had two wives already – instances of bigamy. When Beatrice made a will leaving everything to him, she was found dead in her bath. Smith had discovered a modus operandi that would make him rich and keep him free for more wives. He wed Margaret Lofty in Bath (a terrible irony) and then in London, after the insurance policy, she was found dead in her bath. The father of one of his former women saw the story and told the law. Soon Smith was tracked down and charged. In court, the jury took very little time to find him guilty. He was to be another client for the Rochdale hangman.

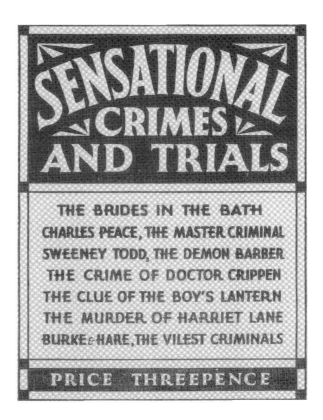

Front page of a booklet.
Anonymous, 1935

Ellis and his new assistant, Edward Taylor, watched Smith as he walked in the yard beneath them, considering his height and weight. Ellis noted that this formerly dashing and healthy man of forty-three looked aged and pale. A drop of six feet eight was arranged. Smith made no confession of murder; he allowed no visitors and seemed controlled, but on the fatal morning he began to fall apart emotionally. The chaplain brought the condemned man out of his cell too early and he was shoved back inside. When eight o'clock approached, he was taken into the charge of the warders and they marched to the scaffold. When Smith saw Ellis he yelled, 'I'm innocent of this crime!' Then, even while the cap was put over his head, he said again, 'I am innocent.' Ellis had no problems 'turning off' that monster.

Ellis's decline and death were indeed very sad. The mental stress and depression that attends on hangmen was seizing him. Around the late 1920s, as the economic depression hit home as well, Ellis felt even more strain. He tried to kill himself in 1924 by shooting himself in the face; but he survived, and of course he had committed a serious crime. His wife found him and rushed him to Rochdale Infirmary. At trial, the magistrates advised him to give up the drink. He was lucky to be merely bound over. Some money was earned by seeing his memoirs into the press: the Thomson group in Scotland paid him for writing *Revelations of My Life*.

But on 20 September 1932, he was drunk and ready to die; he had a razor and was violent towards his family, and he cut himself, dying in his own kitchen.

He had hanged women and teenagers as well as hardened villains and psychopaths. This had all given his constitution enormous strain. The Rochdale hangman was, in spite of all this, a true professional in the kind of work that very few have done well down the centuries. His wife, at the inquest, said that for the last two years, Ellis had suffered from 'neuritis, heart trouble and nerves' – this comes as no surprise when it is recalled just how many hangings he did and in what circumstances. The coroner said, 'I am quite of the opinion that he did this rash act in a sudden frenzy of madness.'

CHAPTER 14

Pierrepoints and the Last Hangmen

he Pierrepoints were to dominate the hanging business between the years 1906–1956. The story begins with Henry (Harry to his friends – though his job might have lost him some of those).

Harry Pierrepoint's brother, Thomas, joined forces to execute Harry Walters on 9 April 1906 at the point when Wakefield's facilities had been refurbished; the death cell and suite (as these areas of prisons were euphemistically termed) were on C Wing. The physical dimensions and technical areas of the scaffold were to receive much attention at various points in the history of hanging; in this instance, the suite consisted of two cells, one having been knocked through so that the condemned man could have some exercise without going out into the general yard.

These death cells were on a second floor landing; at Wakefield the whole place had been purpose built, with the section having a glass top and a beam and chain in a commodious area. A little later, there was to be a controversy about the dimensions of the trapdoor scaffold area, as we now know after the Home Office review in 1920, looking at the tendency of condemned persons hitting their heads as they were hanged (in some prisons). John Ellis was consulted, as we know from papers opened in 2005 in The National Archives, and he said that at Winchester prison in particular, the gallows trapdoors were too narrow. Ellis had recommended that these doors were too narrow and that the walk to the gallows was too long. The Winchester pit was much narrower than the one at Pentonville, for instance. This information, surfacing many years after the execution period, highlight the conditions under which the hangmen worked. Wakefield was clearly aware of the need to address the actual physical space of the scaffold.

In this new workplace the brothers got to work, leaving the rope to hang and stretch overnight, after the weights and rope being ascertained. It was an auspicious start to their partnership; all went very well, Tom was adept at marking the place where the man would stand, and at coiling the noose ready for use at the required height; then both men stood by the cell ready to move their man swiftly to the platform. Walters was pinioned and dropped in seconds.

In an account of Yorkshire hangmen, the question has to arise at some point: what would happen when a man from the hangman's own town was to be executed? The answer to that is illustrated in the case of the Bradford killer John Ellwood. He claimed that he knew Harry well and that when the time came, he would create major problems for the hangman. Ellwood had committed a cool and very public murder. Ellwood had returned to the office where he had formerly worked, in Bradford, and timed his arrival at the time when there would be cash on the premises.

Ellwood had left the firm, Fieldhouse and Jowett, six months previously. He had been in a heated row with his employers and had left under a cloud; it was therefore not hard for the police to show that, as an employee, he would know the routine of the place in a typical week, and would therefore be aware that large amounts of money were brought to the building by the company every Friday. It was hardly going to be a problem for the investigating officers, to find the man who had beaten Tom Wilkinson to death with a poker in that office. There was plenty of blood on Ellwood's clothes when he was arrested, and his pathetic excuse that this was caused by a bleeding nose was not going to fool anyone. The murder scene that day had been observed by a passer-by, to whom Ellwood had vainly tried to lie that he (Ellwood) had only called there to try to obtain his job back and that someone else must have been there in a murderous frame of mind. In court, there was evidence of a letter written by Ellwood saying that he would call that day, but nothing more than that.

The trial at Leeds was spoiled by a technicality, but he was convicted of murder, and then went to appeal. That last-ditch attempt to save his neck was dramatic in the extreme; on 20 November 1908, the applicant for Ellwood, Gregory Ellis, argued that at the trial there had been no motive for the murder satisfactorily stated or explained. A supposed letter from Wilkinson, asking Ellwood to come and discuss the reinstatement had been dismissed and the defence team at the appeal brought this up again. It all came to nothing; the judges were convinced that Ellwood had gone to the office that day with the attention to rob and to kill if necessary.

On 3 December that year, Ellwood had an appointment with the Pierrepoints. The killer had openly bragged that he would create a stir on the fateful day. They had to come up with a contingency plan, and it was decided that two guards walking with the group to the scaffold would stand on planks at either side of Ellwood to restrain him when trouble started. That would mean using the hood and pinions as he struggled or kicked, of course. But the most successful move was that the brothers had the man pinioned in that cell, taking him by surprise. There was no trouble after that, apart from the man's shouts that he was innocent, even directing one call to his hangman, 'Harry, you're hanging an innocent man!' After that, both brothers being convinced that he was not telling the truth, the only other words spoken by Ellwood, seconds before he dropped, were, 'It's too tight.'

Tom, like his brother, had written the usual application, made after John Billington's death at Harry's urging. Tom was interviewed and then went for the training at Pentonville. Of course, he had had some extra tuition from Harry and was well prepared. It seems that Tom was a 'natural' at the work, and he very smoothly adapted to work well with his brother. They were to be severely tested by one of the most

GAS-POISONING SENTENCES.

EARL'S PLAN FAILS TO CONVINCE.

HUMANE HANGING.

COAL gas poisoning for murderers instead of the present method of execution, as advocated by Earl Russell, has been condemned by Lord Justice Atkin.

Earl Russell contended that poisoning would cause less unpleasant anticipation, and there would be no disagreeable spectacle for the onlookers if coal gas were introduced at night into the condemned cell when the convicted person were asleep.

He made this proposal at a London meeting of the Medico-Legal Society, a body composed of doctors, lawyers, and criminologists, which gathers frequently to discuss various aspects of criminal matters.

MENTAL TORTURE.

The current number of the "Lancet" contains many comments of distinguished investigators upon this matter. Lord Justice Atkin, who presided at the meeting, considered that the proposal made by Earl Russell was objectionable, because if the prisoner did not know on which night he were to be poisoned he would lie awake many nights expecting death. If, however, he were forewarned he would certainly not sleep on the given night, and would be slowly suffocated while conscious.

Professor Harvey Littlejohn, of Edinburgh University, declared that death from hanging was absolutely instantaneous. He has been able to examine six recent cases of execution, and as a result contended that the method of hanging adopted in Britain was the most humane of all methods, the operation being performed expeditiously and painlessly, and it undoubtedly caused instant death.

He made an interesting comment on the beating of the heart after the drop had taken place. In most cases the heart continued to beat vigorously for ten minutes, but in one case the heart apparently stopped immediately.

MAHON'S BODY.

Sir Bernard Spilsbury, the famous pathologist, described in detail the examination he made of the body of Patrick Mahon, the Crumbles murderer, in which there were two dislocations of the spinal column.

The poison expert of the Home Office, Sir William Willcox, was another who said that hanging was a painless form of death, and that the hanged man became immediately unconscious, even if convulsive movements were observed afterwards.

For some time there has been public unrest with regard to the method of execution, and there is a feeling in this country that recently all has not been well.

To allay this feeling Lord Justice Atkin suggested that the authorities should provide for a post-mortem examination being made by competent persons, and that the results of the examinations should be published.

The presence of Sir Bernard Spilsbury at the inquest on Mahon and his evidence of the results of the execution appear to have been a step in that direction.

Earl Russell's idea for gas execution.
Daily Sketch, 1915.

bizarre executions ever done, and that was the hanging of Richard Heffernan in Dublin in 1910. The scene that was to emerge was one of tragic-comedy, but very dark comedy nevertheless.

Heffernan had killed a girl called Mary Walker, stabbing her and then telling people that he had seen the murder. But fate had a string of stressful incidents lined up for the Pierrepoints. First, something happened that illustrates the essential need for the hangman to protect the privacy of his identity. For some reason unknown at the time, Harry's name was on the passenger list of the ferry they were taking from Holyhead. People obviously began to take a vicarious and morbid pleasure in knowing who he was; the public hangman was always a figure of intense media interest. Wisely, he was given a private place to hide in for the journey.

The next incident in the Heffernan fiasco was that the condemned had been so unbalanced and determined to flout the hangman that he had set about clawing at his own throat to take his own life. In normal practice, suicide was high on the agenda of a hanging in the planning of the official personnel involved. The man was sedated and put on close guard. The brothers were aware that this was a highly unusual and challenging case. They knew that they would not only have to be acutely aware of the need for precise attention to all safety procedure, but that the victim was likely to do the most unexpected things at any time.

There were priests in attendance and they came to speak with the brothers on the night before the hanging; no doubt there was extended discussion of Heffernan's condition. What Harry must have noticed – and it became important the next day – was that there was a very small space on the trapdoor area by the drop. What happened there the next day was that the condemned man strode into the trapdoor area with a gaggle of priests; he was weeping and praying and kissing the cross. But speed was the first consideration here, and even when Tom did his pinioning well and stood back, there were the priests, still on the trapdoor. There was no alternative: decorum must be broken, and the priests pushed hard out of the way. That's what Harry did, and then down went the lever.

There was controversy in Harry's life not long after this, and it led to his dismissal. The fuss began at an execution in Chelmsford at which the sensitive subject of the hangman's need for drink arose. The fact is that Harry arrived to do the work, with Ellis as assistant, and he had taken a drink or two. It seems that, according to Ellis in a letter to the Prison Commissioners, that Harry had threatened violence to him: ' . . . he threatened what he would do for me, made a rush at me, but the chief warder and gatekeeper intervened and talked to him . . .' Ellis added, 'He is the first person that has ever assaulted me in all my life.'

He said that he and the prison officials felt that Harry had needed drink in order to do execution work. By July 1910, Harry's name was taken from the official list of executioners.

The sign that Harry was being phased out was when Tom stepped into the chief executioner role; this was a job at Holloway. But in 1910, Tom handled his first Yorkshire execution at Armley: this was John Coulson, the most clear-cut and uncomplicated case in Yorkshire murder. Coulson walked around his workplace showing off a summons he had concerning violence to his wife and written on that paper was a statement that he had killed her. Suspicions were aroused and later, a constable found Jane dead at the family house, and Coulson in a deranged state, insisting that he had tried to take his own life. This had happened in Bradford so, again, Tom was in action in his own home town, among people he knew and who knew him.

Tom carried out the execution smoothly and swiftly; the most informative detail in the Coulson case, however, was in the ruse Tom came up with to slip away from the gaol unseen. He and the assistant, William Warbrick, pretended to be journalists and walked through the crowd, notebooks held prominently.

In 1911 Harry tried to put things right with the authorities and he wrote a long explanatory letter to the Prison Commissioners with reference to the Chelmsford affair. Harry included in that letter an implication that Ellis was acting unfairly, to 'do Harry out of work'. He insisted that the report on Chelsmford was a lie and that Harry could have reported Ellis many times for various infringements. The letter ends with a note of special pleading: 'I have a wife and five young children to keep and I can assure you I have had a lot to bear. I should be pleased if you would communicate with the Reverend Benjamin Gregory of the Huddersfield Mission and inquire about me since I came to Huddersfield this last few months.'

There was no reply. Obviously, there was no going back and certainly no second chance. Tom Pierrepoint was now the 'number one' and he had plenty of work in 1913. What is noticeable in that busy year is that normally Ellis and Tom worked separately, with different assistants. On just one occasion – in Worcester in June – Ellis was chief and Tom the assistant. It seems that there was tact and diplomacy at work, and in the Yorkshire hangings in the years from 1913 onwards it was usually William Willis or Albert Lumb who worked with Tom, although Tom did act as assistant on several occasions to Ellis in other counties, notably in the hanging of the famous George Joseph Smith at Maidstone in 1915, as we have seen in the last chapter. Smith, during his trial, said at one point, 'You may as well hang me at once, the way you are going on . . . go on, hang me at once and be done with it.' He was prescient indeed: in a state of complete collapse, he was handled delicately by Tom and Ellis.

Tom was to be hangman until 1946 and his work included several high-profile cases, but his brother Harry was increasingly desperate after his dismissal. What he did in 1922 sums up a tendency in most hangmen at some point in their careers: a need to earn some money from their notoriety. Berry and Binns had certainly done that. But now, Harry Pierrepoint wrote his memoirs for *Reynolds News* magazine. The articles were headed, 'Ten years as Hangman.' It was to be one of the last events in Harry's life, as he died on 14 December 1922, at forty-eight. Arguably, his most poignant execution had a Yorkshire connection, though his victim was a Lincolnshire woman, Ethel Major. He hanged another woman, Charlotte Bryant, at Exeter; both females were sentenced to death for murder by poisoning of their husbands. Just before Christmas 1934, Tom Pierrepoint, assisted by his nephew Albert, hanged Ethel Major at Hull gaol. It was a traumatic experience for all the professionals involved but especially so for the man who had to pull the lever on the scaffold.

Ethel Major, living in Kirkby on Bain, not far from Lincoln, had a husband who was having an affair; she was a complex personality,

Ethel Major.
Laura Carter

tending to express herself in unconventional ways and to some she seemed naïve. She had had a child out of marriage, during the Great War, and then Arthur Major had married her. Ethel was from a rural family; her father was a gamekeeper. In many homes at that time there was strychnine used for various things, along with other poisons (the commonest being arsenic on fly-paper) and when Arthur was taken seriously ill, plain forensic work pointed the finger at Ethel, as she had the means and the motive.

There had been widespread debate on the issue of capital punishment in the early 1930s; one reason for this was the reprieve of a teenager sentenced to hang after a double shooting in Waddingham in Lincolnshire. But also there was the issue of hanging women and also the difficult topic of diminished responsibility. It would be useful and interesting for the public to know how the executioner stood on the matter and, unusually, Tom gave an interview to the *Yorkshire Post* in February 1930. Typically, he was interviewed doing his 'day job' at a foundry. His views were simple and direct: 'I think it would be encouraging people to murder if the death penalty were abolished, but it

Huddersfield gasworks, where Tom Pierrepoint worked at one time. The author

would make no difference to me either way.' Steve Fielding makes it clear that Tom put financial gain before moral debate, however.

His resolve was certainly tested in the Major case. Young Albert had applied for the executioner post in 1931, stressing that his father had taught him well. He was twenty-six at the time and had been brought up largely in Huddersfield, where his father had at times worked at the gasworks. The new Pierrepoint team of Tom and Albert arrived at Hull and made ready to attend to Ethel Major. They would have known the salient points of the case – mainly that a dog had died, as well as Mr Major – but they would not have known how complex the whole affair had been and how it was to influence thought on capital punishment.

The preparation to hang Ethel major must have been highly unusual for Tom. She was a very tiny woman, only just under five feet tall and weighing only 122 pounds. Images of her available show her wearing unflattering glasses and an apron. She had not spoken for herself at the trial and revisions of the case show how terrible was her ordeal, but to the last she was calm, and it appears that she was an 'ideal client' for the Pierrepoints, going stoically to her fate. Young Albert was naturally intrigued by the thought of hanging a woman, as there was an emotional impact involved that needed some reflection. John Ellis spoke at length about his hanging of Emily Swann and Edith Thompson, and he could not resist talking at length about the sense of moral outrage involved in hanging a woman. But apparently Tom Pierrepoint knew the score when it came to the gallows for a woman victim. He reassured Albert that she would be controlled and said, 'I shall be very surprised if Mrs Major isn't calmer than any man you have seen so far.'

For Tom Pierrepoint, two days in January 1919 had him busy in seeing to the death of three soldiers. It had been the tail-end of the war and offences were common as men returned home to face all kinds of relationships problems; there was also a spate of crimes of violence often linked to ex-servicemen. The three hangings involved an assistant we know little about – Robert Baxter.

Benjamin Benson was the first to hang, on 7 January. He had been having an affair with a married woman, Annie Mayne, in Hunslet, Leeds. She was married to Charles Mayne but he had left her when her affair with Benson began and he found them together one day. Benson moved in to live with Annie, but she was a promiscuous type and had other male friends. Benson came home one day and Annie came home with a young soldier, taking him upstairs. Benson went to them and the soldier fled. But after that there was a confrontation and he hit Annie. The argument escalated into extreme violence and Benson took a razor and slashed her throat.

PUNISHMENT, ENGLAND. 433

PUNISHMENT, ENGLAND.

Capital Punishment.

RULES DATED JUNE 5, 1902, MADE BY THE SECRETARY OF STATE FOR THE HOME DEPARTMENT, PURSUANT TO THE PROVISIONS OF THE CAPITAL PUNISHMENT AMENDMENT ACT, 1868,* FOR REGULATING THE EXECUTION OF CAPITAL SENTENCES.

1902. No. 444.

1. For the sake of uniformity, it is recommended that executions should take place in the week following the third Sunday after the day on which sentence is passed, on any week day but Monday, and at 8 a.m.

2. The mode of execution, and the ceremonial attending it to be the same as heretofore in use.

3. A public notice, under the hands of the sheriff and the Governor of the prison, of the date and hour appointed for the execution to be posted on the prison gate not less than twelve hours before the execution, and to remain until the inquest has been held.

4. The bell of the prison, or, if arrangements can be made for that purpose, the bell of the parish or other neighbouring church, to be tolled for 15 minutes after the execution.

5. The person or persons engaged to carry out the execution should be required to report themselves at the prison not later than 4 o'clock on the afternoon preceding the execution, and to remain in the prison from the time of their arrival until they have completed the execution, and until permission is given them to leave.

Chas. T. Ritchie,
One of His Majesty's Principal Secretaries of State.

Whitehall,
5th June, 1902.

* 31 & 32 Vict. c. 24.

The 1902 rules for hanging procedure. HMSO

The following day Tom executed two young soldiers who had murdered a shopkeeper in Pontefract. These men were Percy Barrett and George Cardwell; they had murdered Rhoda Walker at Town End and then pawned some of the goods, even giving some jewellery to Cardwell's mother in Halifax. They went to London, but the pawn tickets, as in so many cases, made it easy to track them down. They said they were innocent, right to the moment they stood on the trap.

The inter-war years were a time of prolonged and heated debate on all aspects of the criminal law. There had been two significant pieces of legislation which influenced homicide decisions, one in 1908 which raised the minimum age of execution from sixteen to eighteen, and the 1922 Infanticide Act which made that offence a variety of manslaughter rather than murder. Then, just before the hanging of Ethel Major, in 1931, there was the Sentence of Death (Expectant Mothers) Act in which pregnant women after giving birth were reprieved. Previously there had been the 'pleading of the belly' which meant that it would be a stay of execution if a woman were pregnant at time of trial.

These were all humane measures, long overdue, but the persistent problems were the nature of insanity in homicide, with the idea of diminished responsibility, and the difficult nature of a whole range of illnesses which an offender might be suffering from.

The Ronald True case of 1922 had an impact on the subject, largely because he had been, in the opinion of the press, 'reprieved by the doctors' and he was wealthy with powerful friends. Harry Pierrepoint, just before his death, commented to the press that there was a gross disparity in that, as another man, with a similar 'crime of passion' was hanged, and he had been poor. The papers talked about 'trial by Harley Street' and the *Evening News* wrote:

> *Mr Justice Avory's terse and mordant comment on leaving the law to Harley-Street experts shows the country where it stands under a Home Secretaryship that says, "I am powerless when the doctors have spoken." All you have to do after a trial, then, is to call in the pathologist, get his certificate, and leave that to confirm or reverse the verdict!*

In 1923, writers to *The Times* on the debate made points which express common feelings at the time; one writer made the point: 'Now what is our machinery? The judge has no option. With due solemnity, he passes sentence of death equally upon the miserable mother and upon the callous ruffian.' Another writer noted that in his opinion, there was 'a growing feeling in the country against capital punishment . . . there is an immense body of silent opinion against it . . .'

The year following there was a deputation to the Home Secretary pressing for the abolition of hanging. The groups involved included the Society of Friends, the Women's Co-operative Guild and the Howard league for Penal Reform. The leading figures were George Lansbury, Major Christopher Lowther and Margery Fry. One of the most strident voices against the death penalty was the campaigner Violet Van Der Elst, a wealthy woman with land and status in rural Lincolnshire who made a habit of driving her large and showy motor vehicle to the prisons where executions were to take place and protest in front of the growing crowds of onlookers.

The hangmen carried on in spite of all the debate and disagreement, but of course, their written statements were valuable documents for both sides. Also in the picture were accounts of the alternatives to hanging, such as the campaign by Elbridge Gerry, founder of the NSPCC, to replace the noose with 'humane' electric death. He wrote many articles on cruelty and capital punishment.

In 1930 there was a Select Committee on Capital Punishment, led by Sir John Power. The crime of murder was the only issue, as since 1838 the only executions had been for that crime. The conclusion was that 'The witnesses felt bound . . . to point out that in their view the risks to which the officers of the law were exposed in the discharge of their duties would be enhanced if capital punishment were abolished' and furthermore, that

'professional burglars and criminals of that type did not normally carry lethal weapons in this country and that was directly attributable to the gallows . . .'

One of the spin-off effects of this new caution and reflection was the nature of recruitment to the ranks of hangman. The Aberdare report of the 1880s had involved the testimonies of medical men such as this, and it was a sobering exercise for all concerned:

I descended immediately into the pit where I found the pulse [of the hanged Man] *beating at the rate of 80 to the minute, the wretched man struggling desperately to get his hands and arms free. I came to this conclusion from the intense muscular action in the arms, forearms and hands, contractions, not continuous but spasmodic, not repeated with any regularity but renewed in different directions and with desperation. From these signs I did not anticipate a placid expression in the face and I regret to say my fears were correct. On removing the white cap about one and a half minutes after the fall I found the eyes starting from the sockets and the tongue protruded, the face exhibiting unmistakeable evidence of intense agony.*

As a result of this, and of Binns's blunders, things began to change. In addition to the expertise of the hangman, after 1913, the medical men present at an execution played their part in ascertaining the length of the drop. There is a difference in the tables of drops for 1892 as compared with 1913; for instance, the average range of weight, say 135–145 pounds, differs by almost a foot deeper drop in 1913. Authorities were taking no chances. There was much more consideration for ensuring a swift exit.

Albert, the last and most celebrated of the Pierrepoint hangman family, applied at a time when the results of these deliberations had an effect on recruitment.

The name of Albert Pierrepoint has almost become the definitive name that follows if the topic of hangmen comes up in conversation; in recent years it has been such a topic, largely because Timothy Spall played Albert in a major motion picture in 2006. That film, and the media interest it generated, gave massive attention to the lives and motivations of the hangmen and it gave audiences something of the Yorkshire context. After all, most of the famous hangmen have been northerners – most from Lancashire or Yorkshire and speculation on why that is the case has always been popular.

Albert's time as chief executioner includes such large slices of crime history as the hanging of Ruth Ellis, the traitor Lord Haw Haw, various German spies, the Nuremburg executions, Derek Bentley, John Christie and Timothy Evans. In all he hanged around 433 men and 17 women and served from 1932 to 1956. He died in Southport in 1992, aged eighty-seven. He wrote his autobiography, but we also have two recent works on his life: Steve Fielding's *Pierrepoint: A Family of Executioners* and Leonora Klein's *A Very English Hangman*.

Albert's progress towards stepping into the shoes of his father and uncle followed the usual course, writing the letter and then being called for interview at Strangeways. He had looked closely at his father's notes on the profession and was fully informed when he went to be considered. When he received his letter of acceptance, it came with a list of rules, and the tone of these is very much a sign of a regime 'under new management' in the sense that there is a great deal of stipulation of conduct and procedure. Most of the rules are concerned with punctuality and discretion; one of the most telling sections reads: 'he [the hangman] should avoid attracting public attention in going to or from the prison, and he is forbidden from giving to any person particulars on the subject of his duty for publication.' The spirit of the rules is in line with the renewed demands for moral probity and sensitivity on the part of the hangmen added to the list.

One man who had recently resigned from the list, Tommy Mann, was still around to advise writers on the Pierrepoints when Klein wrote her life of Albert, and he was one of the select names on the list, only finishing that work because of the demands of his main employment.

For Albert, his first job teamed up with Tom was in Ireland. The two men crossed to Dublin where there was a victim waiting for them at Mountjoy prison. Steve Fielding makes a point that Tom had a revolver and bullets in his belongings before that trip – hardly a feature we might have expected in that trade, but in that instance there had been trouble over in Ireland regarding the killer, Patrick MacDermott, who had been sentenced to die for the murder of his brother. It appears that his motive was to inherit the land where they had a farm, in Roscommon. The journey the hangmen took to Ireland on that occasion was as eventful and tense as anything in a crime novel; they had to make three changes of transport, then take the Holyhead ferry again. As Tom was a good singer, he joined in with a party on the ship, and later there was a gang of people waiting for their arrival in Dun Laoghaire. It was only because a man they had befriended gave them cover and a lift that they escaped trouble. The execution went smoothly, but there was another crowd waiting for them outside the gaol; it seems that Tom was an expert at melting anonymously into a group of people and he did so again, keeping his nephew under his wing. A significant footnote to the adventure (with Harry in mind) is that Tom refused the traditional whisky after the drop, when the corpse was inspected by the doctor and the good job well done celebrated with a drink.

Tom and Albert had another sixteen years in which they acted together from time to time; their joint operations are well documented, but the events which are not so well known are the reprieves. The first case Albert was supposed to watch, simply as an observer, turned out to be cancelled as a reprieve came, and a far more notorious case came along in 1936. This was the story of William Edwards of Bradford. He was sentenced to death for killing his girlfriend but he had severe epilepsy and there was ample evidence of his mental problems to make it a complex case at trial. A highly regarded doctor from Switzerland gave a statement to the effect that there was a case for diminished responsibility for Edwards. He said, 'From the facts put before me, and the examination I have made of the prisoner, I have arrived at the following conclusion, namely, that it is highly probable that Edwards suffers from occasional attacks of epilepsy.' He listed frequent headaches, moodiness and loss of temper, a history of attacks of an epileptic nature, and loss of memory.

On the fateful night, Edwards had gone out with his girlfriend and everything had been fine; they had been to the pictures in Bradford. But later, when they met again, he took out his pen-knife and, according to one statement, 'whirled his arm, not knowing where it fell'. But Edwards had done a similar attack previously. Eventually he was sentenced for murder and was on his way to the Pierrepoints when the reprieve came.

One hanging the two men did do together at Armley was that of David Blake, who had strangled Emily Yeomans in Middleton Woods near Beeston. Emily was a waitress and she lived near Dewsbury Road. The killer went for a heavy drinking session with Albert Schofield (his intended best man) and then went walking with Emily. Blake was hardly discreet in keeping his terrible act quiet; he gave a powder compact belonging to Emily to the wife of a man who had put him up for the night and he made a point of talking about the murder case as reported in the local paper. He was questioned by police and traces of Emily Yeoman's hair were found on him.

There was a chance that he may have been innocent, as police had arrested a man called Talbot and there was forensic evidence to link him to Emily. But it was Blake who went to the gallows.

In the Second World War, naturally there would be spies rather than murders as clients for the Pierrepoints. At Wandsworth in 1941 they had their first such case when they hanged two Germans who had landed near Banff in Scotland; they were Karl Drucke and Werner Walti. They aroused suspicion by their general behaviour and when accosted and searched, Drucke was found to have a pistol, a radio transmitter – and a German sausage. In July 1942, the first Englishman to be hanged for treason was a client of Tom Pierrepoint at Wandsworth: this was George Armstrong, from Newcastle.

In 1941, on 31 October, Albert Pierrepoint acted as chief ex-ecutioner for the first time, and his client was an infamous London villain whose case went to the House of Lords. This was Antonio Mancini, known as 'Babe'. The killing was an ignominious one, simply a fight in relation to the club which Mancini managed, the Balm Beach Club in Soho. Mancini had been threatened after a scrap with a gang of men who he barred, one of whom was Harry Distleman. When they renewed acquaintance in a fight, Mancini had a knife ready. There would obviously be a claim for self-defence on the part of Mancini.

Even though the appeal went to the Lords, the cards were stacked against Mancini; he had a long list of previous convictions for assault and he had carried the knife ready for the encounter. It was at this job, in Pentonville, that Albert met his assistant, Steve Wade. There was no doubt that Albert had learned his trade, as he was already working out the drop when he was asked by a member of staff what might be required. New ropes from the official suppliers were ready, and the hangmen carried out the normal test-drop. This time it was Albert who was the master, with a student, Steve Wade, who was new to the game and needed guidance. They were up at six on the morning of the hanging and Wade prepared the trapdoors. Albert had given close attention to every part of the preparation, all in order to cut seconds off the execution time.

Steve Wade put the cap on Mancini and Albert turned to look at the prisoner; as the noose was put on, Mancini said 'Cheerio.' Albert had certainly impressed the prison staff and his speed and efficiency were noted. He and Wade worked very well together, as Albert's memoirs show.

In Yorkshire, one of Albert's first tasks was to hang Sidney

ROYAL COMMISSION ON

Capital Punishment

1949-1953

REPORT

Presented to Parliament by Command of Her Majesty
September 1953

Royal Commission on Capital Punishment, 1953. HMSO

LONDON
HER MAJESTY'S STATIONERY OFFICE
PRICE 12s 6d NET

Cmd. 8932

Delasalle, who had shot Ronald Murphy at the North Country Camp in February, 1944. This was one of those rare cases in which there was a slight possibility of the killer being in a condition of automatism, which, if proved satisfactorily by medical experts, could constitute a defence and a shift from murder to manslaughter.

Delasalle, a soldier at the North Country camp, was in a very bad mood one day when Flight sergeant Murphy and Corporal Taylor came to inspect the beds in Delasalle's quarters; the man was aggressive and actually challenged Murphy to go outside for a fight. That was the last straw and Murphy put the man on a charge. He did fourteen days of 'jankers'. When he came out, the revenge was vicious and swift; a line of men were queuing for tea when Delasalle appeared on the scene with a rifle. He shot the man several times and was then overpowered.

Clearly, there was no doubt of his guilt, but at the trial in Leeds a Dr Macadam brought up the subject of the possible automatism that may have applied to Delasalle. This is the defence made when it is demonstrated that a killer was in a trance or sleepwalking when a homicide was committed. If so, in this case Delasalle would genuinely have had no memory of what he had done. It all came to nothing; such a defence is extremely difficult to demonstrate conclusively to a jury of course.

The soldier was hanged at Durham in March, 1944.

Another wartime Yorkshire murder that led to work at the scaffold for Albert (and this time with a new assistant, Herbert Harris) was yet another killing by army men; it took place at the *Nags Head* at Clayton Heights, Bradford, in September 1944. Arthur Thompson, a soldier, and Thomas Thomson, were regulars at the pub. Arthur had made it plain to his friend that he was desperate for money, and yet one day he went to the Westwood Hospital and paid off some debts to his cronies. He was doing dangerous and risky things, including going AWOL from the army. He went on a crime spree across the Pennines, but he also did the thing that most often ends up with the police at the door: he sold some of the items stolen from Jane Coulton at the *Nag's Head*.

What Thompson had done was break into the inn and stolen money and jewellery. It seems as though Jane had been woken up and disturbed him, and she had been strangled in her bed. The forensics showed that specimens of a different blood group from Jane were present in the room at the scene where there had been a struggle in the bed. This was group A and tallied with Thompson's blood.

The killer was caught trying to sell another piece of jewellery in Overton. The police were called and the man, with false papers on him with the name of Reid, was arrested. Other items stolen from Jane Coulton were found hidden in the police car in which he was taken to be questioned.

Albert Pierrepoint was by that time an expert in his profession; he had been busy with traitors and was soon to be in demand at the trials of Nazis for war crimes. But first we must recall his execution of one of the most notorious traitors in any nation's history, the so-called Lord Haw Haw, William Joyce. Early in the Second World War, the Nazi regime had established a widespread propaganda network, including the provision of English-speaking staff at radio Berlin. In addition to that, the Germans must have been stunned at their good fortune in

Lord Haw Haw. Author's collection

having an ex-Blackshirt British fascist, William Joyce, working for them with his nickname of Lord Haw Haw. He had said that he would go to Germany (even before the war began) and 'throw in his lot' with them. He was treated with a certain degree of suspicion as he may have been a double agent, of course.

But a man working for Goebbels' propaganda machine supported Joyce, against the odds, and he was accepted. Soon his broadcasts, beginning with 'This is Germany calling' and expressed in a cut-glass accent, were becoming familiar everywhere. He also began writing scripts for other radio outfits which were part of the German initiatives of psychological warfare.

Joyce was born in New York in 1906; his father was Irish and his mother English. At school in Galway he had his nose broken in a fight and that affected his enunciation, giving the nasal quality to his broadcast voice later on; but he was to turn out a fit, athletic man and found an outlet for his aggression and his politic in British fascism. He even led one group of fascists into a confrontation at Lambeth Bath Hall and at that place he was cut along the face and so had a scar – something always prominent in images of him later on.

Naturally, Joyce supported the fascists established under Oswald Mosley and lasted there until 1937, leaving them under a cloud.

Under a threat of internment, he crossed to Germany in August 1939. From there his life and work led inevitably into a life as a traitor to Britain, his last broadcast being made from Hamburg in April 1945. He was arrested and charged with treason and sentenced to death, having been caught near the Danish border. He drew a swastika on the wall of the death cell and was without remorse to the end, even when he knew about the concentration camps.

Joyce's trial at the Old Bailey lasted three days. It was a hard task to demonstrate the offence of treason and in the end, everything depended on the date his British passport expired. As it expired after his first broadcasts, he had committed treasonable offences. He even had his appeal go to the House of Lords. But on 3 January 1946, Albert, assisted by Alex Riley, hanged Lord Haw Haw.

Of course, Albert was very much in demand at the War Crimes trials in Nuremberg. There had been a long period before these trials began, as the great powers and the leaders disagreed at first about the required methods of dealing with Nazis. The crimes were in a range of areas, principally in theft of works of art and, naturally, in the extermination of Jewish peoples and others in their policy of genocide. Churchill at first wanted a select (and large) number of Nazis shot without trial. The American regime considered plans such as converting the whole of Germany into a pastoral economy with no armaments at all. Largely due to the machinations of Stalin and a series of meetings to discuss trials, the long sequence of war crimes trials began and Albert Pierrepoint was to find himself at the centre of a controversy.

Much of this was related to the events developing as part of the retribution given, coming from the understandably deep hatred and vengeance in so many people. George Orwell, in his column 'As I Please' on 9 November 1945, wrote, after seeing a man kicking a prostrate German prisoner, 'I wondered if the Jew was getting any real kick out of this new-found power that he was exercising. I concluded that he wasn't really enjoying it and that he was merely . . . telling himself that he was enjoying it.'

In other words, when the question of a trial came up, the allied powers had to be careful that they were not as barbaric as the Nazi culprits had been in their phase of power. What happened was that a Royal Warrant allowed for the trial of some of the Belsen camp criminals under the military court system. The men on trial included such notorious Nazis as Kramer, who had been in charge at Birkenau when 200,000 Jews were gassed. This particular trial, of the Belsen Nazis, took over fifty days; at the end, the death sentences were passed, most notably including Josef Kramer, Irma Grese and Juana Bormann. Albert was the man to see these sentences carried out, being flown out there from RAF Northolt to Germany. As biographer Leonora Klein points out, there was a media frenzy at Northolt (so much for secrecy and discretion): 'For the first time in modern history, the hangman was officially embraced by the British state.'

Waiting in Hameln were thirteen Nazis. Albert was to be housed away from the prison, but he obviously spent time preparing for the job. In his own autobiography he wrote about this, even to the point of the loud and constant sound of the graves being dug outside. The most challenging part of his role, however, was that he had to weight and study each person – not his common practice in his normal work in Britain. He had a translator and spent time with each one, even with the three women who would be his victims. It was highly unusual for Albert. For one thing, he was aware that the people waiting to die would hear the traps slamming near to them as the first Nazis went to their deaths. Albert decided to hang the women first, singly, and then have double executions after that.

The bare statistics of Albert's work as executioner in the period between the end of December 1945 and October 1948 were that he hanged 226 people, and of these, 191 were Nazi war criminals or other individuals guilty of the capital crime of treason. The controversy was partly to do with something historian Sadkat Kadri notes: 'The executions themselves were reportedly even more unpleasant than such things are by their nature. Several of the men are said to have had their faces battered by the swinging trapdoor as they fell. Some thrashed around for up to fifteen minutes, suffocating at the end of nooses that had been cut too short to snap their necks.' That criticism does not apply to Albert Pierrepoint. He would not have allowed such things. In his own memoirs he writes, ' I came back to the corridor to pinion Klein, then brought him to the execution chamber . . . I adjusted the ropes and flew to the lever . . . This first double execution took just twenty-five seconds.'

It must have been a bizarre experience for Albert to return to 'normality' after that, and to turn up at various English gaols to hang common murderers rather than mass murderers of the Nazi regime. But one of his most significant jobs has a strong Yorkshire connection: the hanging of John Reginald Christie at Pentonville in July 1953. Christie, the beast of 10 Rillington Place, had strangled several women at that address (no longer in existence) and buried them on his property. Christie was born in Boothtown, Halifax, close to the Dean Clough area, and when he moved to London he became a special constable and used his air of authority, along with his supposed medical skills, to lure women to their doom by means of his self-made gassing equipment.

Christie, known in Halifax in his youth as 'Johnny No-Dick' clearly had profound sexual problems which had a deleterious effect on his self-esteem and played a major part in the development of his psycho-pathic tendencies.

A man called Beresford Brown, living near Christie's lair, found a body when he knocked through a wall. From that point, the hunt was on for the killer, and on 31 March, a police constable walking on the embankment near Putney Bridge, questioned a man hanging about, looking dishevelled; although the man said he was one John Waddington, when he took off his hat, the officer saw that he was the wanted man, Christie. He confessed to the killings, stating that he had used a ligature to strangle his victims.

At the trial in June, 1953, Christie's defence put up the argument (only to be expected) that the man was guilty but insane. But that plea was dismissed and he was found guilty of murder. Naturally, with such a notorious client, there was a massive crowd gathered at Pentonville to be present at the momentous time when the 'beast of Rillington Place' would meet his doom. Harry Smith was assisting Albert that day, and as they passed a window from where they could see the crowd Albert said, 'I suppose that's the sort of lot who watched hangings at Tyburn, with blokes selling sweets and hot rum to the crowd!'

Christie went to his death with a sneer on his face; as the hood was slipped on, Albert sensed something, and this, as he explained later, was that 'It was more than terror . . . at that moment I know that Christie would have given anything in his power to postpone his own death.' Christie was close to fainting when Albert moved sharply to send him away, from the trap into eternity.

Albert's last Yorkshire appointment was to despatch a soldier, Philip Henry, who had raped and murdered Flora Gilligan at York in March 1953. This was a particularly repulsive crime; the victim was seventy-six years of age. Henry, who was due to go on active service abroad the next day, was nailed by forensic work, some splinters of wood being found on him, and these matched the wood on the window frame at the house in Diamond Street, York, where the crime was committed. There was also a matching fingerprint found, so Henry had little hope of acquittal and indeed at the trial, after a request by the jury to visit the scene of crime, he was found guilty of murder. Albert stepped into work at Armley, the place where Steve Wade normally worked, to hang Henry.

The Pierrepoint dynasty of hangmen undoubtedly created a great deal of professionalism and pride in their work; Albert is the one from the family whose career has had the most prominence in the media and in biography, and one aspect of that long career that needs to be stressed is that he withstood a huge amount of pressure in all kinds of contexts, from the war crimes work to his responses give to commissions on capital punishment. On top of that he had to carry on acting with restraint, discretion and self-respect when the work he did was repeatedly questioned as attitudes changed. Certainly after the hanging of Ruth Ellis and then with the growing understanding that Timothy Evans had been hanged for a crime he did not commit (his wife having been killed by Christie) there was cause for self-examination and reflection. He had shown the Prison Commission that he could keep up the requirement to show 'complete reticence' as their handbook put it in the 1930s.

Albert's resignation came with a dispute about fees. After the execution of a man called Bancroft in Manchester, Albert wrote to the Commissioners, after the man had been reprieved: 'On returning home I was only paid my out of pocket travelling expenses'. Then, nothing being settled to his satisfaction, he wrote on 23 February 1956: 'In the circumstances I have made up my mind to resign and this letter must be accepted as a letter of resignation. I request the removal of my name from the list of executioners forthwith.'

Albert died on the 10 July 1992, in a nursing home. His former assistant, Steve Wade, had retired through ill health in October 1955 just before Albert's last year in office. Just a year after Albert's resignation, the 1957 Homicide Act, introduced by Sidney Silverman, passed in the Commons, but as Charles Duff put it in his book, *A*

DIANA WITHOUT GLAMOUR
Outstanding in 'most gruesome' film

BRITAIN last night presented the most harrowing picture so far shown at the 1956 Cannes film festival when "Yield to the Night," in which Diana Dors plays a murderess in the condemned cell, was given its world premiere.

The blonde star was cheered by 3,000 people as she left the floodlit Festival Palace in her turquoise car matching her turquoise mink stole and sequin-studded evening gown.

She told reporters: "This is the part I have been waiting for, and it has taken me nearly 10 years to achieve it.

Film experts among the

— as she appears in the film.

— as she is usually seen.

audience of 1,800 producers and technicians from 34 countries described the slowly unwinding tale of a

woman's last days under sentence of death in a British gaol as the most gruesome shown at Cannes.

CONTROVERSY

They said Miss Dors, cast as a woman torn between desire to justify her crime and fear of the price she must pay, gave the outstanding performance of a career so far built on her success as a glamour girl.

They also praised the sensitive acting of Yvonne Mitchell as a prison guard.

Members of the British film industry said the picture, to be shown in London soon, is bound to revive public controversy over capital punishment.

Feature on 'Yield to the Night' – on a murderess in the condemned cell.
Scunthorpe Evening Telegraph

Handbook on Hanging, it got 'short shrift when it went to the House of Lords but there is a deep irony in the fact that hanging was 'suspended' for the whole of 1956. But the man he trained learned well. Wade, from Doncaster, was to have a short period in office, but had some tough trials of nerve and strength.

Steve Wade

Steve Wade comes down to us from one photograph; our image of him is of a man with a drink and a cigarette, the face suggesting someone under pressure, maybe a nervous type. That is not associated with a hangman, of course. What the image does convey is that he was maybe ill when the picture was done. He was not in office long – from 1941 to 1955 – and had to retire through ill health. He died in 1959, having been assistant to both Tom and Albert Pierrepoint. Steve handled twenty-nine hangings as chief executioner, and he had some really difficult cases.

He once said that he 'carried out more executions than I could remember' and that suggests a man who was not necessarily meticu-

Steve Wade.
Laura Carter

lous. He also pointed out that the hanging was a sideline. Indeed it was, because he was in the transport business in Doncaster. If a full biography of him was ever written, the subtitle might read, 'Executioner and bus owner.' When he wrote to the Home Office to offer his services, he was at first refused as he was so young, but Wade must have been determined because he wrote again later and then was accepted. He was placed on a waiting list and given the usual course of instruction, before being appointed deputy to Thomas Pierrepoint.

Wade went to live in Doncaster in 1935 and he established his coaching business in the Waterdale area. He must have had a sense of humour (very dark) because, according to Brian Bailey, Wade tricked Albert Pierrepoint into thinking that both he and Wade were needed to be at the post-mortem of a young man from Burma who had murdered his wife, after they had executed the man. The pathologist involved was the famous Keith Simpson. According to Molly Lefebure, who was Simpson's secretary at the time, Pierrepoint walked into the set-up scene and said, 'If you don't mind, I'd like to take a look at my handiwork.' That hardly seems in keeping with the man, and if he did, he would have seen a fracture dislocation between the second and third cervical vertebrae. Bailey makes the point that such a detail signifies the quickest and 'cleanest' death for a victim of the hangman's art.

Wade's first job as assistant was with Tom Pierrepoint at Wandsworth, where they hanged George Armstrong, a man who spied for Germany, starting that work after contacting a German consul in the USA. He was tried at the Old Bailey, then appealed and after that failed, found himself facing the noose.

But before Steve Wade began his main work in Yorkshire, he had a job with Albert hanging another spy that turned out to be a terrible ordeal. Wade took a few notes on jobs, and a typical one is this one on William Cooper at Bedford in 1940. Tom and Albert were the official hangmen, but Wade must have been there to observe and to learn, because he made these notes:

> William Henry Cooper at Bedford, aged 24. Height, five feet five and a half inches. Weight 136lbs. Drop 8feet one inch. Assisted to Scaffold. Hanged 9 a.m. on Nov. 26 1940.

He notes that the personnel present were 'Pierrepoint, Wade and Allen' but that does not tally with the official record.

As time went on he wrote more, as in the case of Mancini for which he wrote 'Three appeals with the House of Lords.' But the ordeal was to come with the execution of the spy Karel Richter. Richter's records have now been released and we know that his mission was to deliver funds and a spare wireless crystal to another spy. He was given a code and money and also a supply of secret ink and was even briefed on what to say if interrogated. Acccording to some opinions, his arrival on espionage work was part of a 'double-cross ' system which meant that agents were captured and given an option either to work as double agents or to face the gallows.

Richter was parachuted into Hertfordshire in 1941 and it appears that Churchill wanted him executed, as other agents had landed and not been hanged. That might be arguable, but what happened, according to MI5, is that Richter landed on the 14 May and that war reserve constable Boott at London Colney saw a lorry driver talking to a man who turned out to be the spy. Sergeant Palmer of St Albans was informed and came to assist. Richter was taken to Fleetville Police Station and there he showed a Czech passport. When searched he had a ration book, a compass, cash and a map of East Anglia.

Richter was seen by a girl, Florrie Cowley (nee Chapman) who recalls going to visit her divisional campsite, of the guides, at Colney heath and that she and a friend went into a storage hut. There they saw evidence of very recent occupation. She wrote in a memoir,

'We quickly came out to think the situation over. Being war time there were no vagabonds, tramps etc around so who could be living there? We then thought a German spy could have dropped . . .' They were right. Photographs survive of Richter going back to the field with army and police to find his buried equipment. Richter stands in one photograph, pointing, while surrounded by personnel. He was destined to be Pierrepoint and Wade's client on 10 December 1941.

Wade kept notes on what happened that day. It was a horrendous experience for the young hangman, so early in his career. First he wrote, 'Karl Richter, 29, five feet and eleven and a half inches. 172 lbs. Execution: good under the circumstances' That has to be one of the greatest understatements ever written. Richter was athletic, strong and determined to cause the maximum resistance when the hangmen arrived at the death-cell. Wade wrote:

> On entering cell to take prisoner over and pinion him he made a bolt towards the door. I warded him off and he then charged the wall at a terrific force with his head. This made him most violent. We seized him and strapped his arms at rear . . . The belt was faulty, not enough eyelid holes, and he broke away from them. I shouted to Albert 'He is loose' and he was held by warders until we made him secure. He could not take it and charged again for the wall screaming HELP ME.

Things were still very difficult, as the man then had to be man-handled by several warders. Even at the scaffold, Richter fought:

. . . he then tried to get to the opposite wall over trap. Legs splayed. I drew them together and see Albert going to the lever. I shout wait, strap on legs and down he goes. As rope was fixed around his neck he shook his head and the safety ring, too big, slips . . .

Wade's notes have a tone of relief as he writes finally, 'Neck broken immediately.'

At the end of his notes he wrote that he said something to Albert, a comment along the lines of 'I would not miss this for fifty pounds . . .'

Richter actually stated under questioning that he had declined to take a part in the 'double cross system'. He had been a marine engineer and had a child in the USA. He was interned and returned to Germany after trying to return to America. In Germany he was recruited by the Abwehr (the German intelligence and counter intelligence organisation). Nigel West, in his history of MI5, has a coda to add to Steve Wade's terrible memoir:

The grisly scene had a profound effect on all those present, and, indirectly, on some other Abwehr agents. Several months later Pierrepoint and his chief assistant, Steve Wade, carried out an execution at

Moorfield Street, Halifax, where McEwen's victim, Turner, lived. The author

Mountjoy in Dublin. News of Richter's final moments reached Gunther Schutz and his fellow internees . . . Irish warders gleefully recounted the details of the struggle on the scaffold, sending Richter's former colleagues into a deep depression.

In the war years, Wade was also on duty to hang a Canadian soldier who had committed a terrible murder of an old man in Halifax. Mervin McEwen was on the loose, camping out on the large area of Savile Park in Halifax when he befriended Mark Turner, aged eighty-two. Mr Turner lived on Moorfield Street, very close to the park, and he invited McEwen and another man to have a drink at his home. The soldier went back to his hut on the park after that, but Turner was found battered to death on his settee the next morning and McEwen was nowhere to be found. But the killer had been very careless: there were fingerprints found on a whisky bottle and also battledress and badges from McEwen's regiment, the Royal Canadian Corps. Not surprisingly, there was no sign of the killer. He had run away to Manchester and was about to start a new life with a new identity and a partner, a woman called Annie Perfect. He was then known as James Acton. He must have thought that he had a bolt-hole and was surely beyond being traced, but he was wrong.

Something happened that reinforces the view that steady, methodical police work pays dividends, and that even the craftiest villains fall foul of their own arrogance. The Canadian dropped his guard and did something so foolish, it seems amazing that he was caught so easily.

A constable arrived at his new house, simply making routine enquiries, but when he explained who he was, McEwen produced an identity card with the name Mark Turney on it. The officer was smart and suspicious, so he asked for a signature. He had seen that the letter 'r' had been changed to a 'y' and there was something amiss. The change had been done clumsily so it was easily noticed. Amazingly, McEwen signed as Mervin Turney. The game was up.

The killer saw that any attempt to lie his way out of the situation was futile and he gave himself up. His story was that he had indeed gone back to the old man's house in Halifax, cooked some food and drunk some whisky. In this state, he struck Turner as he woke up, claiming that it was not intentional. His main line of thought was that he was intoxicated and could not have planned murder. He failed, and in forty minutes, the jury at Leeds found him guilty of murder. Tom Pierrepoint and Wade hanged him at Armley on 3 February 1944.

From 1947, Wade did several hangings in Leeds, beginning with Albert Sabin from Morley, who murdered Dr Neil Macleod at Topcliffe Pit Lane in Morley in 1947. Sabin had been seen running and getting into the doctor's car in the early afternoon of 21

September 1946. Sabin was just twenty-one, and in his army uniform. At around half past two that same day a shot was heard in the lane.

The doctor was found dead only a short time after his murder, by Harry Philpott as he was walking near to the Topcliffe pit. The scene was like one of Hitchcock's more macabre episodes, as poor Harry followed a trail of blood, then a knife and finally a gun. Then there was the body of MacLeod in a hollow, having been shot three times as it turned out.

The hunt was on for the doctor's car, a Ford V8. It was not a difficult task in those naïve days when occasional, opportunist criminals (unlike the professionals of course) merely took their victim's property and did not think too much about forward planning. Sabin was found in Pudsey, where his car was parked, and arrested. There was also no question of any mindgames or ploys to buy time and cause trouble: Sabin simply confessed to the killing when accosted.

The issue was whether or not this was a murder; but it was ascertained that Sabin took the gun with him when he went to meet the doctor, and that he had at least an intention to rob, and most likely to do grievous bodily harm if resisted. Taking the victim's life was merely one more step away from that, with a related intention of 'malice aforethought'. The only further complication came later when the killer tried to say that the doctor had made sexual advances to him; there were semen stains found on clothing, but they could have occurred just as naturally as part of the shock of death as much as in a sexual encounter, so nothing was conclusive there. Sabin claimed that on the day of the murder, Macleod had said he would give Sabin a lift back to camp, but then had driven to a place where he could make his advances. Naturally, Sabin tried to construct a narrative which culminated in a struggle and consequently that the gun had fired with no intention on Sabin's part to take life. That story did not convince the jury and Steve Wade, along with Harry Kirk, had a client at Armley – just twenty-one and a hardened killer – waiting for them in the death cell in January 1947.

The team of Wade and Kirk were busy in the summer of that year at Leeds. Wade and Kirk did three hangings by the end of 1949 and Wade had another assistant for yet another Leeds execution in that eighteen months. Wade's victims were from that area of life we might call domestic-tragic. Their killings were of women, either known to them or prostitutes. The men waiting for the noose at Armley were invariably killers driven by sexual passion, or aggression while drunk, or of course, a combination of all these. Typical was the case of the sad murder of Edith Simmonite in Sheffield. Edith spent a night enjoying a few drinks in the *Sun Inn* and she had been in company with two men who lived at a nearby hostel – William Smedley being one of them. On the night on which someone murdered Edith, Smedley's bed at West bar had not been slept in. There were sound testimonies to that fact later.

So when Edith's body was found, strangled and after having sex, it was a case of basic police work to find out who she had been with and where she had spent her time that day. The task was made even more straightforward by the fact that she was known to the police as a local prostitute. When questioned, Smedley clearly relied on the man with him to back him up in a lie – that the two men had parted from the woman that night and seen her go into her room. Smedley's tale was not verified by his companion, and so the option open to him then was to invent another suspect. He did this by inventing 'an Irishman' who had ostensibly been in Edith's company. He even claimed that the mysterious Irishman had confessed to the murder to him (Smedley). Smedley had been interviewed twice, and told a plausible tale, so was released on both occasions.

What was also very disturbing and seedy about this case was that Edith's body was found by a young boy. Peter Johnson was out looking for wood in the old buildings in the areas of the city that had received bomb damage when he found the body. He said, 'I looked through the doorway and saw a woman lying face downwards at one end of the room. I ran and fetched Ronnie [his friend] . . . and then we went to tell a bus man.' Edith was only twenty-seven, and she also had been living in a women's hostel in the same West Bar area. Her hostel landlord had not seen her since the Friday, and her body was found on Sunday.

The man must have been at least partially convincing, because he claimed the killer had gone to Rhyl and the police gave Smedley the benefit of the doubt, going with him to Rhyl to try to find the killer. Nothing came of that. Not long after, Smedley told the truth to his sister.

The killer had one more story to tell in order to try to create some kind of desperate extenuating circumstances around the vicious murder. He said that he had had sex with Edith but then she had told him that she had a venereal disease, so this information prompted him to attack her, and he lost control in his rage.

None of this achieved anything that would save him from the scaffold; he was hanged by the Wade-Kirk duo in August 1947. Smedley had been told that he had no chance of an appeal, but in sheer desperation he tried the last ploy – a letter to the Home Secretary asking for a pardon. As Sheffield writer, David Bentley, has written in his book *The Sheffield Hanged*, 'The execution attracted no interest, not a single person being present when the statutory notices were posted outside.'

A hanging at Leeds in March 1950 was one of those cases that once again highlighted the complex moral and legal issues around the execution of young people. Two young men, Walter Sharpe and Gordon Lannen robbed a jeweller's shop in Albion Street and the jeweller decided to fight them. In the struggle, Abraham Levine, forty-nine, was battered during this attempt to save his goods from being stolen by force. He was cracked with a gun butt and still would not let go his hold on one of the robbers. Then two shots were fired and Levine was mortally wounded.

Sharpe was twenty and Lannen only seventeen. They had some imaginative notions, perhaps from gangster films, because they fired their guns into the air as they ran away. Both had firearms and the most tragic footnote to the story is that they went away with no stolen goods at all. Their victim died the next day.

Simple ballistic analysis linked the bullets in Leeds to bullets fired at a robbery in Southport and the villains were tracked down. Under questioning, it emerged that Sharpe had fired the fatal shots. As in hundreds of similar cases, the defence was naturally that the gun went off in the struggle, and that defence failed. They had robbed before, while armed, and they had been reckless outside as well as in the premises.

In court matters were straightforward: as a crime was being committed, firearms were discharged: it was murder. Of course, that led to the inevitable conclusion: the elder man to be hanged and the younger, teenager, to be a guest of His Majesty for a very long time. Their choice of Albion Street, right at the very heart of the shopping centre of Leeds then as now, meant that they were firing guns in the vicinity of passers-by, citizens of all ages, going about their daily business.

But of course, the old discussions came back: there were only three years difference in the two young men, yet the older one was to hang. On the other hand, the older one had fired the gun that killed the victim. The 1908 Act had banned the execution of persons under sixteen, and in 1938 that age was raised to eighteen, after some high profile cases led to prolonged debate.

Walter Sharpe was hanged at Armley on 30 March 1950. Wade and Harry Allen officiated.

Towards the end of his short period in office, Wade had two victims both called Moore. The first, Alfred Moore, was guilty of killing two police officers and so his story made all the papers and provoked those elements of society in favour of retaining the death penalty to insist that for the murder of police officers, hanging should always be the sentence. In the 1957 Homicide Act, there were five definite instances in which hanging should be applied and one was 'Any murder of a police officer acting in the execution of his duty or of a person assisting a police officer so acting.' Moore's killing had done much to put that sentence there.

The double murder took place in the most unlikely of places: the quiet suburb of Huddersfeld, Kirkheaton, at Whinney Close Farm. Even today, this is an area in which older property with ample gardens stand side by side with newer suburban developments, quiet, occupied by families, and on the edge of the town, not far from the fields and smallholdings around Lepton.

In July 1951 Alfred Moore was a smallholder there, keeping poultry. But he also had a sideline in burglary to earn some extra cash. He was evidently not very skilled in his criminal activities and the police soon had him marked for observation. On 15 July the police surrounded his little homestead with the intention of catching him with stolen goods on him or on his property.

It was a stake-out that went badly wrong. In that very peaceful early morning of the Sunday, shots were fired in Kirkheaton and as officers moved around in the dark, trying to communicate and find the source of the gunfire, it was discovered that two officers had been shot: Duncan Fraser, a detective inspector, was found dead, and P C Jagger was severely wounded.

It was learned that Moore was holed up inside his house and it was inevitable that he would eventually be captured. The only glitch in the investigation was that, as a revolver had been used in the killings, a revolver had to be found on the person or the property and that never happened. Moore had a shotgun. But despite the use of a metal-detector, a revolver was never located.

But of course, P C Jagger was still alive so there was a witness to the dreadful events of that early morning. From his hospital bed, Jagger picked out Moore from a line-up. In a stunning piece of bravery and high drama, a specially formed court was formed at the hospital so that Jagger, almost certainly dying, could testify. Moore was tried for murder in Leeds; P C Jagger died just the day after giving evidence. Wade and Allen were busy at Armley once again.

The other Moore was a partner in a car sales company, along with Tom Bramley. They naturally met with other car dealers and one of these was Edward Watson. This terrible tale began with the sale of a faulty vehicle to Moore, sold by Watson at a cost of £55 (in 1954 a large sum). That transaction was to lead to a murder at the darkly fated area of Fewston, near the reservoir in Swaledale, where two more murders had occurred.

It was when the car was sold back to Watson at a loss that trouble started brewing. Moore wanted to get his own back after the dodgy deal. Moore arranged to meet and then drive his enemy to Harrogate to see a vehicle. That was the black beginning of a brutal plan, because Moore had a rifle fitted with a silencer for that journey. He had been careless, though, because he had a spade in the back of his car and that was noticed by others; later that would be very much against him.

Harrogate is only around eight miles from Fewston, along the scenic road towards Blubberhouses (going along the dale finally to Skipton) and in fact Moore had shot his victim five times and then driven out to the desolate spot to bury him. Mrs Watson was obviously worried about her husband's disappearance and police questioned Moore, who claimed that Watson had never turned up for their meeting and jaunt to Harrogate. People knew about both the rifle and the spade, and an officer called Wilby persisted with his questioning of the dealer.

The killer boldly said to the officer, 'You don't think I've shot and killed him do you?'

That was a neat summary of the actual events. Moore grew desperate and he actually tried to take his own life, but then he caved in and confessed, beginning to formulate a tall tale about a fight with the gun and an accidental death. There were lots of anomalies in statements made – things that did not sit easily with the forensic evidence. In court, it became clear that this was a case of murder and Moore was sentenced to hang.

Wade's last hanging was a more mundane case: simply a case of a man killing his wife's mother – the woman who had stood in the way, as he saw it, of his happiness with Maureen Farrell of Wombwell. Her mother, Clara, became an object of hatred for the young man, Alec Wilkinson, only twenty-two years old. On 1 May 1955, Wilkinson had a great deal to drink and worked himself up to a mood of extreme violence and enmity towards Clara Farrell.

Not long after their marriage, Alec and Maureen had been under pressure, and the relationship between Alec and his mother-in-law was one of extreme emotional tension, she was apparently always criticising him and making it clear that he was worthless (at least that is how he claimed to see the situation). On the fateful day when he walked up to the front door of the Farrell's home in Wombwell, he had a burning spite in him and he was in a mood to use it. First he sprang on Clara and punched her and then slammed her head on the floor.

But such was the man's fury that he went for a knife in the kitchen, stabbed her, and then did something that suggests a psychosis as well as a drunken fit: he piled furniture on the woman and set fire to it. Wilkinson left as someone came to try to put out the fire, but later Alec confessed and one of his statements was that he was not sorry for what he had done. There was an attempt to demonstrate provocation, and even a petition to save him, but Wilkinson was found guilty of murder at Sheffield and sentenced to hang. This time, on Wade's last appearance as hangman, when he was becoming too ill to do any more, his assistant was Robert Stewart.

Steve Wade returned to Doncaster and lived on Thorne Road, Edenthorpe. He had been a café proprietor and he operated Wade's Motor Coaches. He retired in 1955 and died just over a year after hanging Wilkinson, on 22 December 1956, at Doncaster Royal Infirmary. The only teasing question about his official obituary is this note: 'Buried at Rosehill Cemetery (unconsecrated) in Doncaster.' He seems to have been a very reticent character. Syd Dernley, who worked with him, said simply, 'Wade was a quiet man and said no more than hello when Kirky did the introductions.'

Perhaps the laconic Albert Pierrepoint said the simplest and best thing about Steve Wade, in his autobiography, *Executioner: Pierrepoint*. When being questioned about his work, he was asked, 'Do you know whether any of those who are at present on the list [the official Home Office list of hangmen] have ever carried out an execution?'

Pierrepoint replied, 'Only one, and he has done five or six. Steve Wade, a good, reliable man.'

All the chief executioners began as assistants after the turn of the nineteenth century. The new 'health and safety' mentality took over and a probationary period was seen as essential. There was no place for the prurient or the sadistic dreamers who formerly applied. Before the new attitudes it had been a case of learning by doing. Marwood was unusual, practising drops with sacks in his home village of Horncastle. Others before the more organised years would not be too concerned about standards and wanted the pay, and of course plenty of drink to steel them to the task in hand.

In the twentieth century it became essential for a new man on the Home Office list to learn by observation and to be properly instructed in all the elements of the job, including appropriate behaviour and tact. We do not have many memoirs of hangmen generally and some of those in print are not very helpful. John Ellis did talk to a 'ghost writer' and there are books by Pierrepoint and by Dernley. But the other assistants are shadowy figures. We sometimes have just a few bare facts about them. The main website source for hangmen lists twenty-one men who worked as assistants in the twentieth century. Of these, four worked in Yorkshire from time to time, but undoubtedly Dernley and Allen have the most interest in terms of Yorkshire-based cases. In the late Victorian period, Thomas Henry Scott of Mold Green, Huddersfield was on the list from 1892 to 1901 and at times was the main executioner. We know that Scott assisted Berry but little else has come down to us. There is one anecdote of Scott, though. When he was working in Ireland (in Londonderry) he was the target of a wild mob who threw rotten vegetables at him as he travelled in a cab to the prison. It seems he was also robbed on one occasion in Liverpool; Steve Fielding tells the tale:

> *On arriving at Lime Street station, he shared a taxi with a young woman of questionable virtue, Winifred Webb, and instead of heading directly for the gaol they chose to cruise around the city for a while. On reaching his destination and after bidding farewell to his companion, Scott discovered that he had been robbed of two pounds, nine and sixpence and a pair of spectacles.*

When Scott stepped into the police station to report that, there was the woman, claiming she had been robbed; she was arrested and of course, it was embarrassing for the hangman, who should have stuck to routine and gone straight to Walton gaol.

Syd Dernley

In Syd Dernley we have a hangman who basked in the notoriety of his trade and was always happy to explain the dark and disturbing secrets of the neck-stetcher's mystery.

Dernley wrote a chatty, darkly humorous autobiography of his life

Syd Dernley.
Laura Carter

as a hangman, from his first interview in Lincoln to his last memories of working with the more famous characters. In later life he showed a macabre interest in the trappings of his trade and was only too pleased to regale the media with his tales.

When Dernley was interviewed in 1994 he was happy to pose for the camera with his ropes dangled in front of him. It was noted then that he had been in office from 1949 to 1954 and that he was 'never given an official reason' for that removal. Syd was from North Nottinghamshire, living in Mansfield when interviewed, and he was patently pleased to show off his equipment and mementos to the interviewer. He displayed his case, with a hood inside, a legstrap, armstrap and a replica noose. The interviewer noted that Syd enjoyed 'gallows humour'.

Dernley even used to have a full-sized working gallows when he ran a shop in Mansfield, something taken from a prison in Liverpool; he noted that he had to sell them. He gave a similar reason to Harry Pierrepoint when asked why he had done the work: 'It was not that I wanted to kill people, but it was the story of travel and adventure, of seeing notorious criminals and meeting famous detectives.' But the usual moral complexities arose in the interview when he was asked about the hanging of Timothy Evans, clearly as it turned out, innocent of the murder of his wife. Dernley said, 'Well, if I helped to kill an innocent man as you seem to be implying, it doesn't worry me one little bit. I did the job I was trained to do, and I did it well.'

Dernley's most interesting Yorkshire connection was, oddly, with a man hanged at Strangeways. Nicholas Crosby had killed Ruth Massey at Springfield Road in Leeds in July 1950. He had cut her throat after taking her home following a night drinking in the *Brougham Arms*.

Crosby had given a story of what he had done to his sister, confessing to the murder, but then changed the tale for the police. He claimed that there had been another man and that he heard a scream after walking away, leaving Ruth and the stranger together. His reply to a direct question about whether he killed the woman or not was 'To be sure sir, I don't know if I did . . . if I did, I don't remember.' He was found guilty of murder and because some execution chambers were being modernised at Armley, Crosby was sent to Strangeways to die. Dernley described the man: 'Crosby was a twenty-two-year-old gypsy . . . he was to give any number of versions as to what happened.'

Dernley worked with Albert Pierrepoint for the job. What became remarkable about this was that, as Dernley recalled, a man came along to Pierrepoint's pub, *Help the Poor Struggler* (in Manchester) with the intention of bribing the hangmen so he could get a picture of a hanging. The man said, 'Look, I've got a business proposition to make to you.' He wanted to get a camera into the whole process.

When Dernley told him it was impossible, the man said, 'No, it's not, we will supply you with a miniature camera, a tiny thing. It's so small you'll be able to wear it on your shirt and it'll be hidden behind your tie until the moment he goes down . . .' Of course, Dernley refused.

One thing we have from Syd Dernley is detailed accounts of the events at his executions. In Crosby's case, he writes well of such things, as in his account of entering the death cell: 'As it turned out, we were right to be worried about Crosby. He was scared out of his wits and when we entered the condemned cell I think he came very, very close to breakdown and hysteria . . .' The killer asked for the straps not to be tied too tightly, so Dernley and Albert made sure that there were warders ready to intervene if anything devious was planned. As Dernley wrote, 'Crosby was down and dead in a split second.' He then notes that two assistants had come along to watch and learn – Doncaster man Harry Smith and Robert Stewart. Dernley commented, ' . . . poor Smith and Stewart! In the corridor they must have heard all the commotion without being able to see what the hell was going on. One look at their faces was enough to tell that it had been quite unnerving . . . not a good job for their first experience of executions.'

Dernley's other Yorkshire tale involves the Hull killer, James Inglis. Inglis is the man who has gone down in the history of hanging as the man who ran to the gallows. Like Crosby, Inglis was hanged in Manchester, in May 1951. This tragic but farcical story from court to gallows began when being asked by the judge if he had anything to say, Inglis said, 'I've had a fair trial from you and the members of your court. All I ask now is that you get me hanged as soon as possible.'

Inglis had been in the army, but there were deep personality problems with him; he had a spell in a mental home before coming to Hull, working in Hessle. He enjoyed his food and he wanted sex from prostitutes. He met Alice Morgan, the daughter of a skipper and had been married but divorced; when she met Inglis she was living near the centre of Hull by the railway station. They went out together for a while and then one day he handed in his notice – one minute's notice – at his work. He spent the day after that drinking with Alice, and they quarrelled over money. When she said that she could earn an easy £5 from any man that night, Inglis snapped and brutally beat her up.

The postman, Alfred Brougham, came to deliver a parcel at Alice's house in Cambridge Street and there was Alice's body on the sofa. She had been beaten on the face and strangled by a silk stocking. Inglis had already attacked a woman – his previous landlady, Amy Gray. He was therefore easy to trace, and he had been seen by a number of people in Alice's company. His story was that he lost his temper, hit Alice and then, 'The next thing I knew, she was dead.' Dernley relates what happened as the police went in search of Inglis: 'At the end, Inglis was pathetic and grovelling. They ran him to ground at Victoria Mansions, the Salvatian Army hostel for homelss down-and-outs in Great Passage Street, a stone's throw from Cambridge Street. He blurted out a confession as soon as Detective Inspector James Cocksworth identified himself.'

There was a reasonable possibility that there could have been a defence of insanity at the trial in Leeds before Mr Justice Ormerod. He had said when arrested that he had gone 'mad' at two places (referring to Amy Gray). In his background there were certain details that might have helped to construct a defence: his maternal grandmother had suffered from insanity and died in a mental home and Inglis's discharge from the army had been ostensibly because of a personality disorder. But there was nothing in that material to persuade the jury that he had not intended to kill Alice Morgan and he must hang.

Dernley has left a detailed account of the man who ran to the gallows; he noted that Inglis in the death cell was playing cards with warders and that he had lost a lot of weight. Albert Pierrepoint was in charge and he knew immediately that Inglis was around 139 pounds and a drop of eight feet would be needed (Dernley noted that was the longest he had ever seen).

Strangely, this bizarre execution was an event chosen for observation by the High Sheriff of Yorkshire. Both hangmen thought that such a visit was very rare and could not explain why it had happened. It was a foreboding for the strangeness to come. After they had eaten breakfast, the two hangmen went to the condemned cell and there was Inglis, smiling at them.

Inglis then turned and raised his hands behind him, ready for them to pinion him; he had done his homework on hanging procedure, it seemed. As Dernley commented, 'He was being so bloody helpful, he was getting in the way.' Then, as the door was opened and he saw the waiting rope, Inglis moved out, ahead of the hangmen; Dernley wrote, 'The man was almost treading on Pierrepoint's heels in his anxiety to get onto the gallows.' He wrote also that the group 'trotted' to the scaffold – a rare event indeed. The High Sheriff must have had a very odd impression of execution.

Dernley was sure that the death of Inglis was the fastest hanging on record, anywhere.

Henry Allen

It could be that the coolest of all hangmen in the modern period was Harry Allen. We know about his professional skills thanks to a memoir written by Robert Stewart. In that book we have a very rare source: an eyewitness to the hangman's trade by a prison officer who was there at the time and has since become a professional writer.

Allen assisted Wade at the hanging of Alfred Moore, the police killer. He also was involved in the hanging of William Lubina at Leeds in 1954; Lubina was a Polish miner who had lodged with a couple called Ball at Springfield Street, Barnsley. He had developed a desire for the wife, Charlotte, and he emerged later that he had written to her expressing his feelings and that he was rejected. She had supposedly hit him at one point.

He lost all control on 25 June and, attacking Charlotte Ball in her home, he stabbed her several times and then ran in a frenzy to another room where he cracked his head repeatedly on a mirror. He had collected a stack of photos of his 'beloved' and clearly had a deep, twisted and unrequited love for her that was in the end a destructive, sick inversion of feelings of any kind of affection.

He had sharpened a knife at work before going to the Ball house that day so there was no doubt that the killing was planned. He was to hang, and Wade and Allen saw him off the scaffold to his death on 27 January 1954.

Allen was a dapper, lively man with flair and style. We have a vivid account of him from ex-prison officer turned writer, Robert Douglas, who was on duty when Allen went to hang Russell Pascoe at Bristol in 1963. We learn much about Allen from a posed photograph of him, taken as he stands by a Rolls Royce, a tall man with overcoat, bowler hat and brolly – every inch the ex-army gentleman.

Douglas wrote of the hangman: 'Allen is gregarious company. A tall, slim man in his late fifties, his hair short, clipped moustache and smart blue suit give him an almost distinguished air. He is a publican in Manchester. For around fifty years he has been number two to the doyen of British hangmen, Pierrepoint.' Douglas recalled that Allen, on the night before the hanging, 'held the floor and regaled us with some of the jobs he and Pierrepoint had carried out over the years'.

Douglas's final note about Allen is that he returned just four minutes after pulling the lever to the officers' mess and picked up the cigarette he had left in the ashtray. He was asked if the man was any bother?

'Good as gold' said Allen.

Allen also hanged the last man to die in Armley – the Hungarian Zsiga Pankotia. That was surely an example of the most clumsy, transparent and thick-headed killing on record, because all Pankotia had done was go to the home of pools-winning market trader Eli Myers. Myers had made the mistake of telling people that he had won the money – well over a thousand pounds – and so invited trouble.

Pankotia went to Myers's home in Street Lane to rob him, but the trader confronted him. Pankotia picked up a bread knife and the two had a long and desperate fight. In that struggle, Myers was fatally wounded. Pankotia ran away, taking the trader's van. He was soon tracked down and arrested, but the real interest in this case was not in the banal and clumsy killing but in the courtroom.

The famous forensic scientist from Leeds University, Professor Poulson, made a statement that Myers had been suffering from a heart complaint. Could he have died as a result of that illness, rather than from the wounds inflicted in the struggle? But that detail was not enough in the end. The jury thought that the killing had happened 'in the furtherance of theft; the act of 1861, laying down the concept of grievous bodily harm applied yet again: such an intent was also murderous and in this case happened during a robbery. Pankotia had to hang.

There had to be some kind of lingering belief that the death could have been from natural causes, however, as the case went to the court of appeal, but no unsafe conviction was stated and the first ruling was confirmed.

The chapel on Lister Lane, Halifax. The author

On 29 June 1961, the gallows at Armley Gaol were used for the last time and Harry Allen, with Harry Robinson, were the last hangmen to work there.

Harry Smith

We know practically nothing about Harry Smith who assisted on various occasions, but we know for sure that he was working with Steve Wade on the hanging of the man responsible for one of the worst, most heinous Halifax killings of the twentieth century: the murder of little Mary Hackett, just six years old, by Albert George Hall, caretaker of the Congregational Church in Lister Lane, Halifax. This was in August 1953, and the search for the missing girl had been the main story in the Yorkshire papers during the days in which the search for Mary grew increasingly desperate. The area around the church was then one of old Victorian villas and wide, leafy lanes. Mary went missing there after going out to play and after twelve days, Scotland Yard were called in, and even blood hounds from Wakefield.

In the end, the case was cracked by old-fashioned Holmesian observation. Hall, as caretaker in the church, had used his cunning to bury Mary's body beneath the crypt and placed under furniture and two opened tins of paint. Superintendent Ball noticed the opened tins and after some time he realised that they were open in all probability to cover another smell. Police began digging down to the crypt under the furniture and there they found little Mary's body. She had been brutally beaten in the face.

There was no evidence directly to convict Hall, but he was watched closely and later he went to a mental asylum where he had once been a patient. The police went to interview the doctor there (it was at Scalebor Park Hospital) and they learned that Hall had given information to the doctor that only the killer of Mary Hackett would have known.

Albert George Hall was tried at Leeds, and of course, with the mental health record being quite solid and documented, it was a difficult case. But after several hours of deliberation, the jury found Hall guilty of murder. Hall appealed, but that failed. Hall simply said to the judge, 'My Lord, I am not guilty of this.'

It did him no good, and he was in the hands of Smith and Wade on 22 April, to be marched to the scaffold and be sent to his death.

In February the next year, the principal debate in the House of Commons was that on the abolition of capital punishment. *The Times* reported:

> *The government will submit a motion asking the House to take note of the report of the Royal Commission under the chairmanship of Sir*

Ernest Gowers. No issue is raised by the Government motion, but the abolitionists will seize the opportunity of trying to persuade the House once more to declare itself in favour of the suspension of capital punishment for an experimental period of five years.

It came in the end, but for one year only. The hangmen, chiefs and assistants, must have thought their incomes and duties under threat of being no longer in demand. The old argument, expressed by John Ellis in interview, 'Hanging is clean. It's the cleanest way of them all for putting them away' was being challenged more widely.

Conclusions

After the hanging of Edith Thompson in 1923, Margery Fry, a social worker, sent a statement to the Royal Commission on Capital Punishment. She wrote: 'I was at that time living in Dalmeny Avenue close to Holloway prison, and as a visiting magistrate was frequently in the prison . . . I offered to visit Mrs Thompson because I thought she might have some messages she might want me to deliver . . . two or three days later I was in the prison and saw the officers . . . I have never seen a person look so changed in appearance by mental suffering as the Governor appeared to be. Miss Cronin was very greatly troubled by the whole affair . . .' Fry was forthright on the subject of what hanging does to the professionals involved.

On the other hand, back in the eighteenth century, a rakish aristocrat called George Selwyn, was a man who loved executions and hangmen to the point of fetishistic idolatry. Selwyn, when rallied by some women for going to see the Jacobite Lord Lovat's head cut off,

Pomp and circumstance of the law: the assize procession at Bodmin. Author's collection

retorted sharply, 'I made full amends, for I went to see it sewn on again.' It was said that he 'could have fondled a hangman'. He even went to see executions in female costume, hoping to experience the kind of thrill the women (like Madame Desfarges) had at a hanging. These two examples show the extreme ends of the spectrum when it comes to understanding the peculiar ambivalence to hangings that may be observed throughout social history.

In the twentieth century, a look at the Home Office figures shows the gradual decline in the percentage of executions in relation to the capital sentences, and there is a marked difference in the years 1900–29 compared with the following years. In the first twenty-nine years of the century, there was the huge number of 664 capital sentences, of which 413 were executed and most of the rest respited (the figure excludes suicides in custody). Then in the years 1930–48 there were 388 convictions and 193 hangings.

Into the 1950s we find a much more open and active lobby across

Selwyn, the fetishistic hanging enthusiast. Author's collection

all areas of the criminal justice system working for reform. In 1961 two Penguin Special publications confronted the vexed questions of the hanging of innocent people and the controversial topics of police investigations such as forced confessions and the actions following intense pressure to arrest and convict. On top of that, in the 1950s there had also been the issues of hanging women and teenagers, coming to a head with the execution of Ruth Ellis in 1955. Leslie Hale, who wrote one of the two special editions, said of the Ellis case, 'Blakely . . . wanted to break off the relationship with her in favour of another woman and she shot him one day in the street as he got out of his car, having waited for him, intending to do so. She acknowledged all this. It was pleaded on her behalf that she was hysterical and emotionally immature. She had recently had a miscarriage. No appeal. Hanged at Holloway Prison.' In that book, *Hanged in Error*, Hale presented six full case studies of executions in which there was considerable doubt about either the act itself or about police investigation.

Arthur Koestler, who wrote the other book, *Hanged by the Neck*, printed what he called a 'Creed for abolitionists' and in that document he said, 'The hangman is a disgrace to any civilized country. Doctors have made it clear (through the BMA) that they would never take over the executioner's job by administering lethal injections. We depend,

Another instance of the fascination: John Lee, the man they could not hang. He survived three attempts and went free.
Chris Wade

Where some of the condemned ended: a flogging yard, felons buried beneath, Port Arthur.
The author

for our professional killers, on the type of person who voluntarily applies for the job of operating a rope and trapdoor.'

The notorious hangmen in Britain have been the men who generally did the work primarily for the second income, or in some cases for cash that made their main income, monopolising on the secondary perks such as selling clothes and receiving payments from the surgeons for dissection corpses. Some have done the work for social and religious reasons, as with Marwood, who spoke of ridding the world of 'vermin'. Most have suffered terribly for their careers, both mentally and physically. What cannot be denied is the fact that most survived the trauma of their first hanging, and went on to do more, either fortified by drink or possessed by some strange crusading zeal against felons.

The main issues and debates were always about the hanging of women or young people. All but Albert Pierrepoint were involved in such cases. The account I have given of Ethel Major and Edith Thompson highlights these issues. Regarding young people, the turning point came after the 1931 fiasco of a killing by a seventeen-year-old boy of his uncle and aunt in Lincolnshire. The various commissions and enquiries into the hanging of women and children happened over a long time span, and it is disgusting, with the knowledge of hindsight, to look back on that slow progress to enlightenment.

Finally, what about women hangpersons? Apart from a case in America in which a female sheriff almost had to do a hanging herself, there has only been one notorious such figure. This was a woman known as 'Lady Betty' who operated in County Roscommon between c.1780 and 1810. She was educated, though she was poor, and the story goes that her dark side expressed itself when she once murdered a stranger who came to her home for shelter. Then, under arrest, her career followed that of man early executioners: she was allowed to live if she hanged others. She reputedly said, 'Spare me and I'll hang them all!' This is a tale somewhere between history and folklore, but it does illustrate the nature of hanging in the popular imagination. Something in the reader of dramatic and sensational history wants to know what judicial murder was really like.

Perhaps what sums up the nature of these notorious hangmen and their morbid attraction is the maxim by Sebastien Chamfort: 'This morning we condemned three men to death. Two of them definitely deserved it.' But if we really want a case study in the reasons for notoriety among executioners, we can look to French history for one of the worst ever. This was the executioner Perruchon, called 'La Lanterne' because during the French Revolution he hanged anyone who was even a suspicious looking character from the nearest lamp-post. After that he tended to marry the young women who came to plead for their relatives' lives. He was not worried about bigamy.

Notorious implies a bad or questionable reputation. That can easily be said of any one of the hangmen in the preceding stories. I hope these case studies have opened up a most strange and terrible profession – one we abandoned in 1964 when Peter Allen was executed at Walton gaol and Gwynne Evans, on the same day, was hanged in Manchester.

Acknowledgements

Many thanks to Pamela Brooks, Chris Wade, Laura Carter and Andy Tennick for help with Illustrations and pictures. Also, credit to the Museum of London for permission to use the 'Last Dying Speech' image and to HMSO for the two illustrations included. Thanks also to Cheshire and Chester Archives and Local Studies, for the Burrows illustration, ref: ZCR 60/4/16.

Bibliography

ote: I am particularly indebted to writers Steve Fielding, Geoffrey Abbott and Derek Yarwood for their excursions into hangman history. In addition, writers for the various popular magazines listed here helped to open up some of the more obscure tales.

Main Sources

Syd Dernley with David Newman, *The Hangman's Tale* (Hale, London), 1989

John Ellis *Diary of a Hangman,* (True Crime Library, London), 1997

Forshaw (ed) *Yorkshire Notes and Queries* (Baines, Bradford), 1880

Harold Furniss (Ed.) *Famous Crimes: Police Budget Edition,* (Furniss, London), 1910

Henry Hawkins *Reminiscences of Sir Henry Hawkins* (Nelson, London), 1909

Pierrepoint, Albert *Executioner: Pierrepoint* (Hodder and Stoughton), 1974

Strahan J A *The Bench and Bar of England* (Blackwood, Edinburgh and London), 1919

Robert Patrick Watson, *A Journalist's Experiences of Mixed Society* (Macmillan, London), 1880

Punch in Wig and Gown (Educational Book Co. London), 1910

Steve Wade Mss. In Doncaster Archives: DZ MZ 65/1, letter from Churchill and notes on several cases including the Richter material.

Secondary Sources

Books

Abbott, Geoffrey *William Calcraft, Executioner Extra-ordinaire* (Eric Dobby: Barming), 2004

Abbott, Geoffrey *Execution: A Guide to the Ultimate Penalty* (Summersdale, London), 2005

David Bentley, *The Sheffield Murders 1865–1965* (ALD Design and Print, Sheffield), 2003

Bland, James *The Common Hangman: English and Scottish Hangmen before the Abolition of Public Executions* (Zeon, London), 2001

Pauline Chapman *Madame Tussaud's Chamber of Horrors* (Grafton, London), 1986

Davies, Owen *Murder, Magic, Madness* (Pearson, Harlow), 2005

Michael Diamond *Victorian Sensation: the spectacular, the shocking and the scandalous in Nineteenth century Britain* (Anthem Press, London), 2003

William Donaldson *Rogues, Villains and Eccentrics* (Phoenix, London), 2002

Jack Doughty *The Rochdale Hangman* (Jade Publishing, Oldham, 1998

Charles Duff *A Handbook on Hanging* (1928 1st ed, (Tempus, Stroud), 2006

Oliver Cyriax *The Penguin Encyclopaedia of Crime* (Penguin, London), 1993

Earl of Birkenhead *Famous Trials* (Hutchinson, London), 1930

Stewart P Evans *Executioner: The Chronicles of James Berry, Victorian Hangman* (Sutton, Stroud), 2004

Steve Fielding *Pierrepoint: A Family of Executioners* (London, Blake), 2006

V A C Gattrell *The Hanging Tree: Execution and the English People* 1770–1868 (O U P, Oxford), 1994

Jonathan Goodman *The Daily Telegraph Murder File* (Mandarin, London), 1993

Kelly Grovier *The Gaol: The Story of Newgate* (John Murray, London), 2008

Christopher Hibbert *The Roots of Evil: a social history of crime and punishment* (Sutton, Stroud), 2003

Robert Jackson *The Chief: the biography of Gordon Hewart, Lord Chief Justice of England, 1922–40* (Harrap, London), 1959

Steve Jones *Yorkshire: The Sinister Side Book 1* 1850–80 (Wicked, Nottingham), 2004

Sadakat Kadri *The Trial: A history from Socrates to O J Simpson* (Harper, London), 2006

Ludovic Kennedy *10, Rillington Place* (Gollancz, London), 1961

John Laurence *A History of Capital Punishment* (Sampson, Low and Marston), 1940

T J Leech *A Date with the Hangman* (True Crime Library, London), 1998

Klein, Leonora *A Very English Hangman: The life and times of Albert Pierrepoint* (Corvo, London), 2006

Peter Linebaugh, *The London Hanged* (Verso, London), 2003

Lewis Lyons *The History of Punishment* (Amber Books, London), 2003

Frank McLynn *Crime and Punishment in 18th Century England* (Routledge, London), 1989

Edward Marjoribanks *Famous Trials of Marshall Hall* (Penguin, London), 1950

Thomas Leman Rede *York Castle* (J Saunders, York), 1829

Rowe, John G *The Scaffold and the Dock* (Mellifont Press, London), 1938

George Ryley Scott *The History of Corporal Punishment* (Torchstream, London), 1938

Templewood, Viscount *The Shadow of the Gallows* (Gollancz, London), 1951

Donald Thomas *The Victorian Underworld* (John Murray, London), 1998

George Theodore Wilkinson *The Newgate Calendar* (1st edition, 1828, Sphere Books, London), 1991

Derek Yarwood *Cheshire's Execution Files,* (Breedon Books, Derby), 2007

Periodicals and reports

Robert Douglas, 'The Hangman Lights a Cigarette . . .' *The Mail on Sunday,*
    29 May 2005
'Pierrepoint the Hangman Faced the Axe' *Daily Express,* 1 June 2006
Gerald D Robin 'The Executioner: His Place in English Society' in *British*
    Journal of Sociology 15.3. (1964) pp. 234–253
Illustrated London News
Journal of the Police History Society
Lincolnshire Gazette
Murder Most Foul
Punch
The Times Digital Archive
True Crime
True Detective
The Death Penalty in European Countries (Council of Europe, 1962)
Courts of Criminal Appeal (annual)

Web Sites

Back to Billington families in Lancs. www.users.bigpond.com/telglen
York Castle Prisons: www.richard.clark32.btinternet.co.uk/york
The British Female Hanged ditto
Paul R Williams The Ultimate Price: The Unlawful Killing of English Police
    Officers (See: www.murderfiles.com)

Index